Eating well for under-5s in child care

Practical and nutritional guidelines

Second Edition

By Dr Helen Crawley

Acknowledgements

The Caroline Walker Trust would like to thank the Food Standards Agency for funding the updating of the *Eating Well for Under-5s in Child Care* report.

This second edition of the report was written by Dr Helen Crawley. Thanks are due to all those who were involved in the production of the 1998 edition of this report, particularly Anne Dillon-Roberts and the other members of the Expert Working Group (see below).

Thanks are also due to all those who kindly reviewed this second edition, in particular: Jamie Blackshaw and colleagues at the Food Standards Agency, Anne Dillon-Roberts, Helen Glyn-Davies, Judy More, Richard Watt and Martin Wiseman. Special thanks also go to Gemma Hoffman for her help in preparing the sample menus in chapter 6.

Members of the Expert Working Group

These are the members of the Expert Working Group which produced the first edition of this report. Their affiliations are as at 1998 when the first edition was published.

Anne Dillon Roberts (Chair)	Trustee of the Caroline Walker Trust
Diane Brown	Operations Director, Apetito Services, Apetito Group
Chris Dallimore	Principal Registration and Inspection Officer (Children), Sefton Borough Council
Pauline Emmett	Head, Nutrition Team, Avon Longitudinal Study of Pregnancy and Childhood (ALSPAC), University of Bristol
Gill Haynes	Chief Executive, National Childminding Association
Dr Margaret Lawson	Senior Lecturer in Paediatric Nutrition, Institute of Child Health, London
Morag MacKellar	Head of Nutrition and Dietetics, Central Scotland Healthcare NHS Trust
Margaret Mason	Task Chair for Quality, Registration and Inspection, National Private Day Nurseries Association
Maggie Sanderson	Principal Lecturer in Nutrition and Dietetics, University of North London, and Chair of the Caroline Walker Trust
Jane Thomas	Lecturer, Department of Nutrition and Dietetics, King's College, London
Dr Richard Watt	Senior Lecturer, Department of Epidemiology and Public Health, University College London

Advisers

Professor Dame Barbara Clayton	Honorary Research Professor in Metabolism, University of Southampton
Professor Aubrey Sheiham	Professor of Dental Public Health, Department of Epidemiology and Public Health, University College London
Ann Robinson	Early Childhood Unit, National Children's Bureau
Marion Witton	Chair, National Heads of Registration and Inspection Units

Observers

Dr Petra Clarke	Department of Health
Dr Jennifer Woolfe	Ministry of Agriculture, Fisheries and Food

Secretariat

Dr Helen Crawley	Writer and researcher
Rosie Leyden	Editor, Wordworks
Sarah Ivatts	Administrator

Foreword

The Caroline Walker Trust is dedicated to the improvement of public health through good food. Established in 1988 to continue the work of the distinguished nutritionist, writer and campaigner Caroline Walker, the Trust is a charity which undertakes specific projects as a result of grants and donations. A major part of our work is to produce expert reports which establish nutritional guidelines for vulnerable groups. *Eating Well for Under-5s in Child Care* was originally produced by the Trust in 1998, and has been widely used in public health nutrition since that time.

The impetus for the original expert report came from a recognition that increasing numbers of under-5s were spending long periods of time in child care outside their own homes – in local authority or private nurseries, with childminders, or in other forms of child care. This continues to be the case, and while there has been a significant increase of interest in the importance of eating well among the early years sector, the need for clear, evidence-based information for this group remains essential.

There is evidence that the diets of under-5s in the UK are too low in vitamins A and C, too low in iron and zinc and, for some groups of children, too low in vitamin D. Children's diets also contain too few fruits and vegetables, too much of the type of sugars that most contribute to tooth damage, and too much salt. However, until the publication of the first edition of this report in 1998 there were no nutritional guidelines for food prepared for children in childcare settings across the UK. Recent work in Scotland has produced food-based and nutrient-based standards for use in nursery care which are to be welcomed and the Caroline Walker Trust (CWT) urges all areas of the UK to make clear, nutrient-based standards for under-5s in child care a mandatory part of the framework of care we offer. Nutrient-based standards pioneered by CWT have been adopted for school lunches across the UK and we hope that in other areas of public life, where there is a duty of care to those for whom food is provided, there will be recognition that nutrient-based standards are the simplest and most flexible way of ensuring people eat well. We believe that nutrient-based standards are simple and manageable and in chapter 6 we give a detailed explanation of how they have been calculated and why we encourage their use.

Healthy eating and physical activity are vital for proper growth and development in childhood. Those who provide child care are in a unique position to have a positive influence not only on the nutritional intake of these children but also on the knowledge and attitudes the children have towards food and a healthy lifestyle. We have been very encouraged and impressed by the support and enthusiasm of those who provide child care. They clearly recognise the important role they can play in encouraging healthy development through good food. We hope that this second edition of our report will be used as the basis for the promotion of healthy, balanced diets for the under-5s and that our new, more comprehensive nutritional guidelines are accepted as standards for children in child care.

Joe Harvey
Chair of the Caroline Walker Trust

Contents

Chapter 1
Summary and recommendations

Summary

*This report deals with children up to their fifth birthday. The term **infants** applies to children up to 12 months. The term **under-5s** applies to 1-4 year olds – ie. children from the age of 12 months up to their fifth birthday. The term **carers** applies to staff working in child care and early years settings including local authority and private nurseries, and childminders.*

Healthy eating and physical activity are essential for proper growth and development in childhood. To help children develop patterns of healthy eating from an early age, it is important

We are eating our lunch
Siân, aged 5

that the food and eating patterns to which they are exposed – both at home and outside the home – are those which promote positive attitudes to good nutrition.

Growing children need plenty of energy (calories) and nutrients to ensure they grow and develop well, and they need to eat a good variety of foods, including lots of fruits and vegetables, to make sure they get all the other important dietary components they need. A good appetite will usually make sure they get enough energy from the food they eat. However, there is evidence[1] that:

- the diets of children under 5 in Britain are:
  - too low in vitamin A
  - too low in vitamin C
  - too low in iron
  - too low in zinc, and

- their diets contain:
  - too much of the type of sugars that most contribute to tooth damage, and
  - too much salt, which can contribute to higher blood pressure.

In addition, some children in the UK have low vitamin D status which can lead to poor bone health.[2]

Intakes of meat, fish, vegetables and fruit are generally low. An increase in the intakes of these foods would help to ensure that children have the right amounts of vitamins, minerals and other dietary components for healthy growth and development.

Eating is an important part of everyone's life. Encouraging children to eat healthily does not mean denying them food they enjoy. Healthy eating is about getting a varied, balanced diet and enjoying lots of different foods.

Under-5s in child care

The number of children who spend some time being cared for outside the family home has risen dramatically in recent years. In 2005 it was reported that there were over 1.5 million registered childcare places in England compared with around 637,000 in 1997 [3] and of these 21% were with childminders, 52% in day care nurseries and 24% in out-of-school clubs. (Child care provision in Scotland, Wales and Northern Ireland is summarised in chapter 2.) Day care providers therefore supply an increasing proportion of the total food eaten by a considerable number of children across the UK, many of whom will be under 5 years of age.

The way forward

In 1998 the Caroline Walker Trust identified a need for clear, practical guidelines which encourage healthy eating among the under-5s in child care. With the support of the Department of Health, the Trust brought together an Expert Working Group to produce nutritional guidelines which were published in the first edition of *Eating Well for Under-5s in Child Care*. This second edition, which has been supported by the Food Standards Agency, provides updated guidance and more comprehensive nutrient-based standards. These indicate the proportion of energy and nutrients that should optimally be provided during child care. Specific nutrient-based standards are given for food prepared for:

- **1-4 year olds** in full-day or half-day child care, or for those having individual meals and snacks while in child care

- **1-2 year olds** in full-day or half-day child care, or for those having individual meals and snacks while in child care, and

- **3-4 year olds** in full-day or half-day child care, or for those having individual meals and snacks while in child care.

The nutrient-based standards are shown and explained in chapter 6. Information on nutrition – which readers may find helpful in interpreting the nutrient-based standards – is given in chapter 3. Chapter 6 also gives some food-based guidance for menu planners as well as some sample menus which meet the nutrient-based standards. These will give readers an idea of how the standards can be translated into practice. Additional practical information on how the standards can be achieved can be found in *Eating Well for Under-5s in Child Care: Training Materials.*[4]

This report also gives recommendations about food choice and food service and about the importance of physical activity. The provision of a well balanced diet to infants and under-5s is crucial to children's health and wellbeing. The Caroline Walker Trust recommends that the nutrient-based standards and other recommendations contained in this report should become standards for child care and that they should inform those who inspect and register childcare provision.

Recommendations

The following recommendations apply to 1-4 year olds (ie. children aged between 12 months up to their fifth birthday), unless otherwise specified. Separate recommendations for infants up to the age of 12 months are given on page 12.

Nutritional guidelines

1 Nutrient-based standards for food for under-5s in child care are given on pages 65-68 of this report. These should become standards for child care across all settings.

2 Government departments should include reference to these nutrient-based standards in all guidance and legislation affecting child care.

3 Government, local authorities and other providers such as Sure Start and Children's Centres should include nutrition and nutrient-based standards in development plans for children under 5 in child care, and in plans for early years services and education.

4 The recommendations in this report should be used as part of the training guidance to all those who inspect nurseries, crèches, out-of-school care and childminders.

5 All those who inspect childcare services in the UK should monitor the nutritional standards of the food served in the childcare and other early years settings they visit. Inspectors' reports should include comments on food and nutrition. Any childcare setting that does not meet the standards should seek advice from a registered dietitian or registered public health nutritionist.

6 Childcare and other early years settings should be required, as part of the registration process, to demonstrate that they are committed to providing food which meets the standards outlined in this report.

7 Inspectors should look for management commitment to good nutrition and encourage childcare settings to engage in suitable nutrition training for all staff. Nursery owners, managers, caterers, childminders and others responsible for early years services should seek appropriate information and training on how to meet the nutrient-based standards.

8 NVQs, SVQs and the Certificate in Childcare and Education (CCE) are important training opportunities for carers and other early years staff. Qualifications for those caring for under-5s should contain an appropriate section on nutrition and healthy eating which allows students to understand the nutritional guidelines in this report.

9 The European Commission should take account of the nutrient-based standards in this report when looking at European-wide nutritional standards for under-5s within the Community.

Eating for health

10 Children should be encouraged to eat a varied diet. They should eat foods from each of the four main food groups every day. The four main food groups are:
- bread, other cereals and potatoes
- fruit and vegetables
- milk and dairy foods, and
- meat, fish and alternatives such as eggs, pulses (peas, beans and lentils) and soya.

A varied diet is associated with better health as it is more likely to contain all the nutrients the body needs.

11 Fruit and vegetables are particularly important for good health. Under-5s should be encouraged to taste at least five different fruits and vegetables a day.

12 Vitamin C is important in maintaining good health and may have a role in helping the body to absorb iron if both nutrients are present in the same meal. Under-5s should be encouraged to eat foods containing vitamin C at meals – for example most fruit and fruit juices, potatoes, broccoli and other green vegetables, tomatoes and peppers.

13 It is recommended that children up to the age of 5 years should receive vitamin drops containing vitamins A, C and D. This is the responsibility of the parents or guardians but carers could provide information to parents and guardians about where to find out more about them.

14 The iron intake of children under 5 is lower than currently recommended and there is evidence to suggest that low iron status is common in this age group. Under-5s should therefore eat a diet that is high in iron-rich food such as meat, poultry and fish, as well as fruits and vegetables. (Meat and meat dishes are also a good source of zinc.) Children who do not eat meat should have a varied diet containing foods such as cereals, pulses (peas, beans and lentils), vegetables and fruits.

15 The intakes of the type of sugars in the diet which most contribute to tooth decay are higher than recommended among the under-5s. If children have sugary foods, these should be given *with* meals rather than as snacks between meals. Children do not need sugary foods such as sweets, chocolate, soft drinks or honey for energy. Starchy foods – such as potatoes, bread, rice, pasta and yam – are better sources of energy (calories) as these foods contain other important nutrients too.

16 It is important that the under-5s get enough energy (calories) for growth and development. While adults and children aged over 5 are encouraged to eat a diet that is high in starchy foods and low in fat, younger children on this sort of diet may not have the appetite to eat enough food to provide all the nutrients they need. Carers should therefore be sensitive to the needs of children who are fussy eaters or small eaters and ensure that these children are offered a good variety of food that they will accept.

Physical activity and outdoor play

17 Children should be encouraged to be physically active and carers should timetable periods of activity into the children's daily routine throughout the year. Physical activity helps to ensure that children eat enough food and get all the nutrients they need. It also builds up muscle strength and overall fitness, develops physical skills such as balance and coordination, and provides a release for children's energy.

18 It is essential that there is outdoor space where children can play, or access to an outside area such as a garden, park or other safe open space. Exposure to summer sunlight in outdoor play helps children to maintain their vitamin D status. However, childcare settings should have a 'sun policy', with guidelines on how long children can remain outdoors in strong sunshine, and on the use of protective clothing such as sunhats, and a sun screen. All under-5s should be appropriately supervised at all times while outdoors.

19 Children in child care should have access to toys for active play – for example balls, hoops and skipping ropes.

Drinks for 1-4 year olds

20 Children should be encouraged to drink tap water if they are thirsty. Water quenches thirst, does not spoil the appetite, and does not damage teeth.

21 Milk is a good drink for 1-4 year olds. Whole cow's milk is suitable as a main drink for most children from 12 months of age. Semi-skimmed milk can be introduced gradually after the age of 2 years, provided that the child is a good eater and has a varied diet. Skimmed milk is not suitable as the main drink for children under 5 years of age.

22 Diluted fruit juice is a useful source of vitamin C. Children should be encouraged to have a glass of diluted fruit juice with their main meal or with breakfast as this may also help the body to absorb iron.

23 Children should be discouraged from having fizzy drinks and squashes (including fruit squashes and fruit juice drinks), including diet, non-diet and low-sugar varieties, as these can erode the tooth enamel and contribute to tooth decay. Also, they provide little in the way of nutrients, and children who drink them frequently may have less appetite to eat well at mealtimes.

24 If children are given soft drinks (such as squashes) containing the intense sweetener saccharin, these should be diluted more than they would be for an adult or older child – for example, 1 part squash to at least 10 parts water.

25 Children who bring their own drinks to child care should be encouraged to bring a plastic flask or a lidded plastic cup containing an appropriately diluted drink. Many ready-to-drink cartons of squashes, fruit drinks and fruit juices have a high sugar content and cannot be diluted if they are drunk straight from the pack.

26 Tea and coffee are not suitable drinks for under-5s as they contain tannic acid which interferes with iron absorption.

Dental health

27 If children are having sugary foods and drinks, these should be given with meals rather than between meals. This is because children's first teeth are prone to decay if they are frequently in contact with sugars. It is important to reduce both the frequency and the total amount of sugar and sugary foods that children eat.

28 To help the healthy development of teeth, children should not be given sweet drinks (such as fruit juice, squashes and other soft drinks) in a bottle or dinky feeder. An open cup or beaker which does not require the child to suck should be used if these drinks are given with meals.

29 If a child uses a dummy or comforter, it should never be dipped into sugar or sugary drinks, as this can contribute to tooth decay.

30 Some soft drinks which claim to have 'no added sugar' still contain sugars which are harmful to the teeth. Diet drinks, both fizzy and still, can also be harmful to the teeth. This is because they may be acidic and erode the dental enamel, especially if sipped frequently. The use of these drinks should be avoided.

Food hygiene and safety issues

31 Carers should always wash their hands with soap and water before preparing food or helping children to eat, and after changing nappies and toileting children. If carers use a handkerchief while preparing food, they should wash their hands before continuing.

32 Children's hands should always be washed with soap and water before meals and snacks, and after going to the toilet.

33 Carers need to be aware of the requirements of the Food Safety Act. Some carers may need to complete a Food Hygiene Certificate course. Further information on this can be obtained from the local authority's environmental health department, or from its registration and inspection unit.

34 Carers also need to be aware of food safety issues such as storage of food and use of leftover food, and thorough cooking or heating of foods. Several useful publications are available from the Food Standards Agency (see Appendix 5). Carers should obtain and follow the advice in these. Some of the main points for carers are given in chapter 5.

35 Children under 5 should never be left alone while they are eating, in case they choke.

See also *Food hygiene and safety issues for infants* on page 13.

Organisation of mealtimes and snacks

36 Breakfast is a particularly important meal and fortified breakfast cereals can make an important contribution to daily vitamin and mineral intakes. Parents and guardians should work together with carers to ensure that children have breakfast, either at home or in child care.

37 Children need to eat regularly and it is recommended that the timing of meals and snacks is organised with the aim of ensuring that children eat regularly.

38 Children need nutritious snacks between meals. The best snacks are those which are low in added sugar. A variety of snacks should be offered including fruit, vegetables, milk, yoghurt, any type of bread, and sandwiches with savoury fillings.

Sustainability

39 Food purchasers should consider the environmental impact of their food and drink choices and where possible buy local food in season and food from sustainable sources.

Creating the right atmosphere and encouraging social skills

40 Meals can be times of pleasant social sharing. It is good practice for carers to sit with children during meals and snacks. It is important that what the carer eats and drinks provides a good role model for healthy eating.

41 Mealtimes offer an opportunity to extend children's social and language skills. Children can learn from the carer about table manners, and can practise their speaking and listening skills. To encourage this, distractions such as television are best avoided during mealtimes.

42 Children aged 2-4 years should be allowed to serve themselves during meals as this may encourage them to try different kinds of foods. Finger foods of all kinds, particularly fruit and vegetables, will encourage children under 2 years of age to feed themselves and try new foods. Child-sized utensils, crockery, tables and chairs may also make it easier for children to serve themselves and learn to eat independently.

43 Children should be allowed to make their own food choices. If a child refuses a food or meal, the carer should gently encourage them to eat, but children should never be forced to eat. To minimise food refusal, it is important to ensure that a variety of foods are offered.

44 Some children may eat slowly. It is important to ensure that all children have enough time to eat.

Learning through food

45 Food can be used in a variety of educational ways, for example to teach children about food sources, nutrition, health, the seasons, growing cycles and other people's ways of life. Learning how to choose and enjoy many different nutritious foods in early childhood can provide the foundation for a lifetime of wise food choices.

46 Carers should involve children in preparing food and laying and clearing tables.

47 Holidays, festivals and religious occasions provide a valuable opportunity for children to learn about different cultures and special events and the variety of foods associated with these events.

Involving and listening to parents and guardians

48 A real partnership between parents or guardians and carers should be fostered. This could include:
- making menus available to parents, and
- giving parents adequate notice of any changes to meals, food choice or any other aspect of food provision, and allowing them to comment on and discuss the changes before they are introduced.

49 Carers should give parents or guardians clear information each day about what food has been eaten and if their child has eaten well. Even older children may not be accurate in reporting what they have eaten.

50 Carers should ask parents or guardians about any special dietary requirements their child has before the child starts attending the childcare setting. Parents of children who are on special diets (for example a gluten-free diet), or who have food allergies are responsible for providing the carer with information about the food choices available to their child, and parents and carers should jointly prepare a dietary management plan.

51 Carers should seek advice from parents and guardians if they are serving food which the carers themselves are not familiar with. Such food should not only contain the right ingredients but should look and taste right too.

52 Carers may wish to remind parents of the importance of giving vitamin drops to under-5s. Vitamin drops containing vitamins A, C and D are available free to children up to 5 years old in certain low-income families. Parents can get more information from their health visitor or GP, or from www.healthystart.nhs.uk.

Equal opportunities

53 All children, and their parents or guardians, should be respected as individuals, and their food preferences and religious requirements should be accommodated.

54 When planning food provision and menus, carers need to consider children who have special needs. Some children may have particular dietary requirements or may need specific help with eating, both of which are outside the scope of this report. Parents or guardians and carers may find it useful to contact support groups associated with the child's particular disability or need.

55 Carers should positively encourage both boys and girls to participate in all activities, including food-related activities such as cooking.

56 All that children bring with them to their place of child care – their race, gender, family background, language, culture and religion – should be valued in order for children to feel accepted and accepting of themselves. It is therefore important to value the contributions which different cultures and nationalities make to the variety of foods eaten in the UK today.

Infants (children under 12 months)

The Expert Working Group recognises that many infants under the age of 12 months enter child care. Guidelines on infant nutrition are given in chapter 4 and are summarised here.

Drinks

1 Breast milk is the best food for infants. Carers should support breastfeeding mothers and encourage them to continue providing breast milk. Mothers who are breastfeeding and who may wish to feed their baby in the childcare setting should have warm, private facilities made available to them.

2 If expressed breast milk is not provided, infants should be given an appropriate infant formula.

3 Babies who are bottle-fed should be held and have warm physical contact with an attentive adult while being fed. Wherever possible, babies should be fed by the same person at each feed while in child care.

4 Babies should never be left propped up with bottles as this is both dangerous and inappropriate to babies' emotional needs.

5 From 6 months of age, infants should be introduced to drinking from a cup or beaker, and from the age of 12 months, they should be discouraged from drinking from a bottle.

6 Cow's milk is not suitable as a main drink for infants under 12 months. However, whole cow's milk can be used as an ingredient in weaning foods – for example to moisten mashed potato.

7 If drinks other than milk or water are given – for example baby juices or baby drinks – these should be diluted with at least 10 parts water and should be confined to mealtimes. Because of the risk to dental health, children over 6 months should not be given these drinks in a feeding bottle. Water given to children under 6 months should be boiled and cooled first.

8 Adult-type soft drinks or 'diet' drinks, tea and coffee are not recommended for infants.

See also *Dental health* on page 10.

Weaning (from 6 months)

9 Infants under 6 months should not be given the following foods: foods containing gluten (such as bread, pasta or chapatis); nuts and seeds (including peanuts, peanut butter and other nut spreads); eggs; raw or cooked shellfish, shark, swordfish and marlin; citrus fruit and citrus juices; foods containing plant sterols; or honey.

10 Salt should not be added to foods for infants.

11 Naturally sweet fruits (such as apples or bananas) can be used to sweeten foods rather than adding sugar.

12 Artificial sweeteners should not be added to foods for infants.

13 Soft cooked meat, fish and pulses (for example peas, beans and lentils) are important foods to include in the diet from 6 months.

14 It is important to offer a variety of flavours and soft textures. Between 6 and 12 months, food should be given which allows the infant to learn to chew and accept a wide variety of food textures.

15 If using commercial weaning foods, follow the manufacturer's instructions carefully.

16 Eggs given to babies or toddlers should be cooked until both the yolk and the white are solid.

17 Because children in the first year of life are following individual feeding and sleeping patterns, it is recommended that these are not disrupted but wherever possible integrated into the carer's timetable for the day.

18 It is recommended that children up to the age of 5 years should receive vitamin drops containing vitamins A, C and D. This is the responsibility of the parents or guardians but carers could provide information about where to find out more about them.

Food hygiene and safety issues for infants

19 Expressed breast milk provided for babies in child care should be clearly labelled with the child's name and the date, stored in a refrigerator and only used for that child. Any expressed milk left over at the end of the day should be returned to the parent or guardian.

20 Wherever possible, formula milk feeds should be made up fresh for each feed, using boiled water that is hotter than 70°C. (This means water that has been boiled and left to cool for about 30 minutes.)

21 If the carer is making up infant formula, it is preferable if it can be made in a separate milk preparation area.

22 If at any time bottles of milk or infant formula are heated, a microwave should not be used as the contents can become very hot even though the container still feels only warm.

23 Bottles and teats for infants under 6 months of age should be thoroughly cleaned and sterilised. The teats of bottles for older infants should be thoroughly cleaned.

24 If dummies or comforters are used, they should be thoroughly cleaned and sterilised for infants under 6 months, and thoroughly cleaned for older infants. These recommendations also apply to dummies or comforters which are dropped.

25 If the carer is serving food from a can or jar and the child is unlikely to eat all the contents, a portion should be spooned into a separate dish or container before serving it to the child. Any unused portions should be stored according to the manufacturer's instructions. (If there are no instructions, the safest option is to throw the unused portion away.) If food is served straight from the jar and the child does not finish it, the remainder should be thrown away.

26 Any uneaten food which parents have brought in should be returned to them at the end of the day.

See also *Food hygiene and safety issues* on page 10.

References

1 Gregory JR, Collins DL, Davies PSW, Hughes JM, Clarke PC. 1995. *National Diet and Nutrition Survey: Children Aged 1^1/2 to 4^1/2 Years. Volume 1: Report of the Diet and Nutrition Survey.* London: HMSO.

2 Shaw NJ, Pal BR. 2002. Vitamin D deficiency in UK Asian families: activating a new concern. *Archives of Disease in Childhood*; 86: 147-149.

3 Ofsted. 2006. *Quarterly Childcare Statistics. 31 December 2005.* Accessed from www.ofsted.gov.uk/publications/index.cfm?fuseaction=pubs.displayfile&id=4148&type=pdf

4 Crawley H. 2006. *Eating Well for Under-5s in Child Care: Training Materials for People Working with Under-5s in Child Care.* London: Caroline Walker Trust.

Chapter 2
Why nutritional guidelines are needed

Healthy eating and physical activity are essential for growth and development in childhood. To help children develop healthy eating patterns from an early age, it is important that the food and eating patterns to which they are exposed – both at home and outside the home – are those which promote good health and positive attitudes to good nutrition. This chapter describes the current diet of under-5s and food provision for under-5s in child care, and explains why nutritional guidelines are needed.

I play football
Imogen, aged 4

The diet of under-5s in Britain

Growing children need plenty of energy and other nutrients to ensure they grow and develop normally. A good appetite will usually make sure they get enough energy from the food they eat, but there is evidence that children under 5 in Britain are consuming diets higher in the type of sugar that damages teeth than is currently recommended.[1] In addition, the intakes of some vitamins and minerals have been found to be lower than the levels which are likely to fulfil the nutrient needs of most children. Intakes of vitamin A, vitamin C, iron and zinc in particular have been found to be low among a considerable proportion of children under 5.[1] Intakes of meat, fish, vegetables and fruit are generally low. Increasing intakes of these foods would help to ensure that children have the right amounts of vitamins and minerals for adequate growth and development.

Under-5s in child care

The number of children under the age of 5 spending some time being cared for outside the family home has risen substantially as an increasing number of mothers of young children return to the workforce. There are about 3 million children in the UK below compulsory school age and many of these children are cared for in a number of childcare settings including day nurseries, nursery schools, playgroups, with childminders, and in crèches, with au pairs, private nannies, relatives and friends. In addition some under-5s are in early education in both nursery classes and reception classes. The mix of provision of child care has changed substantially in recent years with providers in the public, private and voluntary sectors responding to government initiatives to increase the number of childcare places available through the National Childcare Strategy. Since 1997 parents have been given financial support for child care through the Childcare Tax Credit and the childcare element of the Working Tax Credit and currently more than 55% of the total childcare costs are paid for by Government and private companies and 45% – over £3,000 million a year – by private individuals.[2]

Child care in England, 2005[3]

Childminders

Registered childminders	71,500
Number of places	321,200

Full-day care*

Number of providers	12,900
Number of places	553,100

Sessional day care**

Number of providers	9,900
Number of places	241,100

Out-of-school day care

Number of providers	10,300
Number of places	361,400

Crèche day care

Number of providers	2,700
Number of places	45,700

Early education and primary schools[4]

Number of places for 3 year olds	538,800
Number of places for 4 year olds	577,300

* Full-day care facilities provide day care for children under 8 for a session which is a continuous period of 4 hours or more. This includes day nurseries, children's centres and some family centres.

** Sessional day care provides care for children under 8 for a session which is less than a continuous period of 4 hours in any day, where children attend for no more than five sessions a week.

Data from Ofsted on registered childcare providers and places showed that over 1.5 million places were available in England in 2005 (see *Child care in England, 2005,* below). The largest childcare providers are those offering full-day care and sessional day care (periods of less than 4 hours of continuous care). There has been an increase in the number of private sector day nurseries and a decrease in childminder places since 1997.[2]

In Scotland in 2005 there were 263,000 pre-school age children served by 6,100 childminders and 4,717 childcare and pre-school education centres of which 711 were private nurseries.[5] In Wales in 2005 it was reported that there were 72,856 registered childcare places for under-8s, 15% of them provided by childminders.[6] In Northern Ireland, 9,197 places for under-5s were registered with day nurseries and 18,065 places with childminders in 2005.[7]

The type of child care used by parents or guardians of the under-5s depends on what is available and what they can afford, and may change as the child gets older. Parents may choose nursery schools or pre-school playgroups to socialise and stimulate their children before schooling begins, rather than primarily as a form of child care. In many cases there is a combination of these forms of care: for example, a childminder may look after a child during parental working hours when the child is not at nursery school or playgroup.

It is estimated that there are approximately 350,000 people working in the early years workforce.[8] The cost of child care has increased substantially in the last few years with the average cost of a full-time nursery place in England for a child under 2 in 2005 being £141 per week, although costs are very varied across the country.[9]

Food provision in child care

Although parents or guardians have the main responsibility for providing adequate and appropriate food for their children, day care providers supply an increasing proportion of the total food eaten by children in their care. There is a lack of published work on food provision in the UK under-5s day care sector. The current evidence available suggests that there is a wide variation in the quality and quantity of food provision in childcare settings but there is increasing evidence of good practice.

In 2006 Ofsted carried out a survey into food served in 110 childcare settings: 64 childminders and 46 day-care providers.[10] The inspectors judged that the majority of providers offered a healthy and balanced diet for children but some weaker providers were also identified. Particular concerns in some settings were infrequent serving of fruit and vegetables, lack of variety in snacks served, offering sweets as rewards, and the lack of integration of food served with discussions about healthy eating.

A survey published in 2005 carried out among 168 childcare providers in West Yorkshire[11] found that only half of nurseries and a quarter of childminders offered fruit and vegetables at main meals every day. In this study only 14% of nurseries and 21% of childminders offered calcium-rich foods at main meals, and about half provided meat every day. While childcare providers in this study saw themselves as responsible for promoting a healthy diet, many had had no training in eating well and current guidance was perceived as vague. This study also highlighted tensions between some childcare providers and parents on issues around food and concluded that all nursery staff and childminders should have access to carefully designed advice on nutritionally appropriate food and drink services for under-5s that they could also share with parents.

A study in Dundee looking at food provision in nursery school classes, child and family centres and independent providers[12] concluded that the food served to children in full-day care provided only about 50% of their energy needs and was low in vitamin C and iron. Data from the ALSPAC survey in Bristol on the food and nutrient intakes of 3 year olds[13] reported that, when the nutrient intakes of meals provided by parents and meals provided by other carers were compared, there were little nutritional differences, suggesting that food in child care often mirrors that offered in the home and is therefore likely to contribute to the higher than recommended intakes of sugars and lower intakes of fruit and vegetables observed.

Since the first edition of *Eating Well for Under-5s in Child Care* was published in 1998, new standards have been introduced for children in full-day child care, sessional child care, crèches, out-of-school care, and with childminders. These standards are used by those inspecting childcare facilities through the appropriate regional agencies of the UK. The standards for England published in 2001 are summarised in Appendix 1. National Care Standards for Scotland published in 2002 can be found at www.scotland.gov.uk /library5/education/ncsee.pdf. National Care Standards for Wales published in 2000 can be found at www.csiw.wales.gov.uk. The Caroline Walker Trust welcomes these new standards but believes

that further support, guidance and training are needed for the inspectorate, and for early years workers, to help them interpret what 'healthy and nutritious' meals and snacks means in practice. *Nutritional Guidance for Early Years*,[14] published in Scotland in 2006, provides practical support to all those working in the sector to meet the Scottish National Care Standards. The Caroline Walker Trust hopes that this *Eating Well for Under-5s in Child Care* report will offer additional information to providers across the UK and that both this report and the training materials[15] which accompany it will be the basis of guidance in this sector for England, Wales and Northern Ireland.

Across Europe, nutritional standards for food provided in nurseries, kindergartens and other non-school settings are used in Austria, Denmark, France, Italy and some parts of Belgium and are followed by most local authorities in Sweden.[16] In Italy all children in child care eat food that has been prepared on the premises by trained staff and cooked to nutritional standards set by the health ministry. Staff eat with the children, who are allowed to be involved in food preparation, and there are strong links between food activities and food provision. Parents are consulted about menus and pay the equivalent of about £2 for a meal through their nursery fees. In many parts of Europe it is well accepted that children learn about a healthy way of life through daily practice and pleasant eating experiences.

Those who provide child care for the under-5s are in a unique position to have a positive influence not only on the nutritional intake of those children but also on the knowledge and attitudes children have towards food and a healthy lifestyle. A

successful approach to food intake requires that those providing child care have a commitment to good practice as well as an appropriate nutrition policy. In 2003 the report *Every Child Matters*[17] saw a new focus on quality services for children in the UK. In 2004 a 10-year strategy for child care was announced which aims to work towards national provision of the highest quality child care in the world.[18] The Caroline Walker Trust would like to see the right of every child to good food to be a significant part of this new vision.

The Caroline Walker Trust believes that every child has the right to good food, and that this should be part of the vision for high quality childcare services in the future.

Aims of this report

In 1998 the Caroline Walker Trust identified a need for clear, practical and nutritional guidelines for food provided for under-5s in child care. With the financial support of the Department of Health, the Trust brought together an Expert Working Group to produce the first edition of this report. A list of Members of the Group is given on page 2. This second edition updates the information provided in the 1998 report and extends the nutrient-based standards to reflect new recommendations made since 1998 as well as to reflect new evidence on the nutritional needs of under-5s.

The aims of this report are:

- To provide clear, referenced background information about the relationship between good nutrition and health and development among infants and children under 5.

- To provide practical guidelines to enable local authorities, caterers, nursery owners and managers, childminders, cooks/chefs and others responsible for providing food for infants and under-5s in child care and other early years settings, to develop suitable menus which achieve a good nutritional balance and variety.

- To act as a resource document for those working for better standards of nutrition for infants and under-5s in child care and other early years settings.

This report deals with children up to their fifth birthday. The term **infants** applies to children up to 12 months. The term **under-5s** applies to 1-4 year olds – ie. children from the age of 12 months up to their fifth birthday. The term **carers** applies to staff working in child care and early years settings including local authority and private nurseries, and childminders.

Who the report is for

The main audiences for the report are:

- Those agencies who contract, register, monitor and inspect nurseries, childminders and other childcare and early years settings (the Early Years Directorate of Ofsted; the Scottish Commission for the Regulation of Care [Care Commission] and Her Majesty's Inspectorate of Education [HMIe]; Department of Education Northern Ireland Inspection Services; and Estyn, the office of Her Majesty's Chief Inspector of Education and Training in Wales).

- Directors of Education and Directors of Children's Services and Children and Young People's Strategic Partnerships

- Children's Trusts and Centres, and Healthy Start and Sure Start teams

- Owners, managers, catering staff, local authority staff, childminders, teachers and other carers in environments providing child care for infants and under-5s

- Parents and guardians of infants and children under 5 who will be using childcare facilities outside their own homes

- MPs, MSPs, MEPs (Members of the European Parliament), civil servants, writers and journalists who may wish to know more about aspects of the nutritional needs of infants and under-5s in child care.

The provision of food to infants and under-5s is crucial to children's health and wellbeing. The Caroline Walker Trust hopes that the nutrient-based standards contained in this report become accepted standards and recommends that all those involved in the care of infants and under-5s should adopt all the nutritional guidelines outlined here and put the recommendations into practice.

References

1 Gregory JR, Collins DL, Davies PSW, Hughes JM, Clarke PC. 1995. *National Diet and Nutrition Survey: Children Aged 1$^1/_2$ to 4$^1/_2$ Years. Volume 1. Report of the Diet and Nutrition Survey.* London: HMSO.

2 National Audit Office. 2004. *Early Years: Progress in Developing High Quality Childcare and Early Education Accessible to All.* London: TSO.

3 Ofsted. 2006. *Quarterly Childcare Statistics. 31 December 2005.* Accessed from www.ofsted.gov.uk/publications/index.cfm?fuseaction=pubs.displayfile&id=4148&type=pdf

4 Department for Education and Skills. 2006. *Provision for Children Under 5 Years of Age in England: January 2006 (provisional).* Accessed from www.dfes.gov.uk/rsgateway/DB/SFR/

5 Scottish Executive. 2005. *Pre-school and Childcare Statistics 2005.* Accessed from www.scotland.gov.uk

6 Care Standards Inspectorate for Wales. 2005. *CSIW Annual Report 2004-2005.* Accessed from www.csiw.wales.gov.uk

7 Information on childcare places in Northern Ireland for the year ending 31st March 2005, accessed from www.publications.parliament.uk/pa/cm200506/cmhansrd/cm060306/text/60306w14.htm

8 Cameron C. 2004. *Building an Integrated Workforce for a Long-term Vision of Universal Early Education and Care.* London: Daycare Trust.

9 Daycare Trust. 2005. *Childcare Costs Survey.* Accessed from www.daycaretrust.org.uk

10 Ofsted. 2006. *Food for Thought: A Survey of Healthy Eating in Registered Childcare.* Accessed from www.ofsted.gov.uk

11 Moore H, Nelson P, Marshall J, Cooper M, Zambas H, et al. 2005. Laying foundations for health: food provision for under 5's in day care. *Appetite;* 44: 207-213.

12 Wrieden WL, Farley K, Anderson AS. 2001. *Food in Early Years. An Audit of Food Provision in Nursery School and Classes, Child and Family Centres and Independent Sector Partner Providers in Dundee. Final Report to Tayside Health Board.* Dundee: Ninewells Hospital Medical School.

13 Emmett P, Rogers I, Symes C and the ALSPAC Study Team. 2001. Food and nutrient intakes of a population sample of children in the South West of England in 1996. *Public Health Nutrition;* 5: 55-64.

14 Scottish Executive. 2006. *Nutritional Guidance for Early Years.* Edinburgh: Scottish Executive.

15 Crawley H. 2006. *Eating Well for Under-5s in Child Care: Training Materials for People Working with Under 5s in Child Care.* London: Caroline Walker Trust.

16 Children in Europe. 2006. *An Appetite for Life: Young Children, Food and Eating.* Accessed from www.childrenineurope.org

17 HM Treasury. 2003. *Every Child Matters.* London: HM Treasury.

18 HM Treasury. 2004. *Choice for Parents, The Best Start for Children: A Ten Year Strategy for Childcare.* London: HM Treasury.

Chapter 3
Nutrition and 1-4 year olds

This chapter provides the basic nutrition information needed to understand the nutrient-based standards for under-5s in child care given in chapter 6 of this report. It looks at energy (calories), protein, fat, carbohydrates, fibre and some of the important vitamins and minerals needed by the under-5s. It outlines why they are needed, how much children need, and whether they are getting enough or too much based on current scientific evidence.

The following information applies to 1-4 year olds (ie. children from the age of 12 months up to their fifth birthday), unless otherwise specified. Information on infants up to the age of 12 months is given in chapter 4.

Nutrient-based standards are expressed in terms of the amounts (both maximum and minimum) of individual nutrients needed for good health. Most foods contain a number of different nutrients so it is the *balance* of different foods within a person's eating pattern which determines whether the recommendations for 'healthy eating' are met, rather than whether a person is eating particular foods. It is important that children are given varied diets if they are to obtain all the nutrients their bodies need. How children can achieve the balance of nutrients they need from the food they eat is considered in chapter 5.

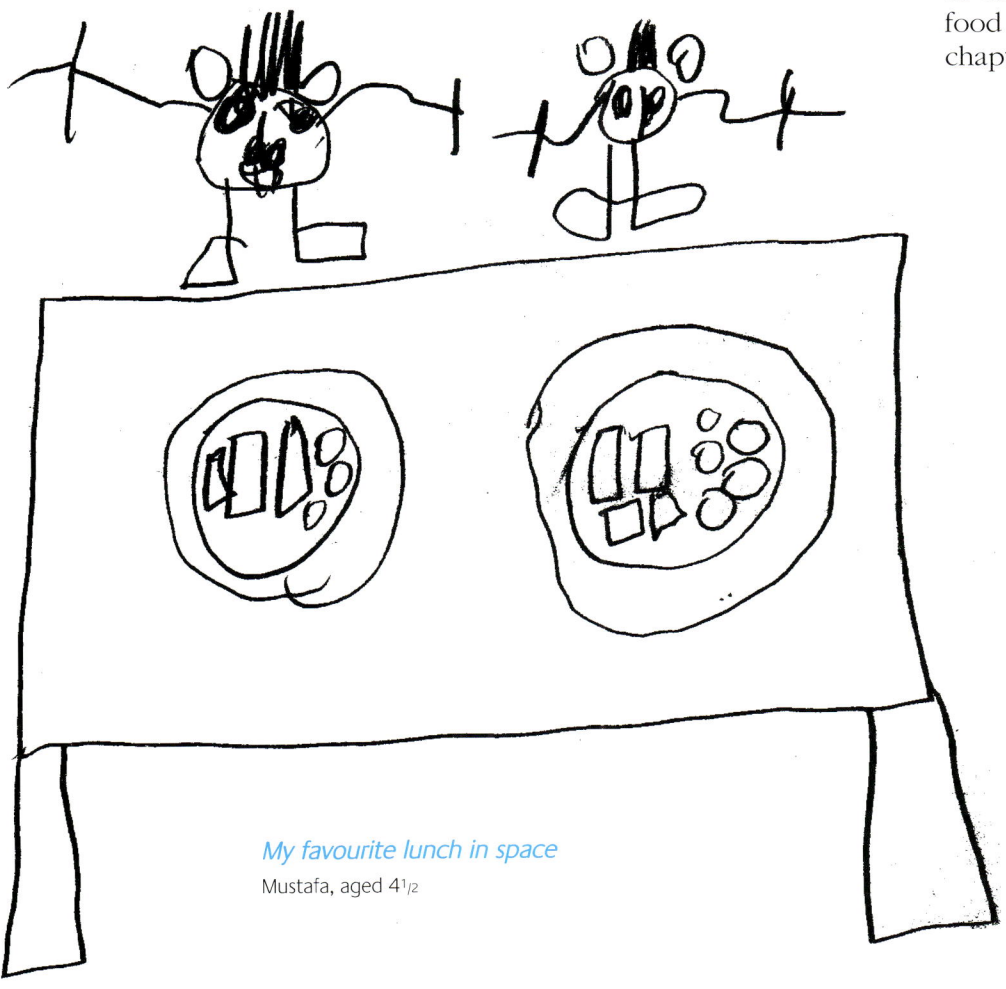

My favourite lunch in space
Mustafa, aged 4$\frac{1}{2}$

Energy (calories)

Why children need energy

Children need a certain amount of energy (calories) to enable them to function and be active. The body gets energy from fat, carbohydrate and protein (and in adults from alcohol), but most energy needs are met by fat and carbohydrate.

Children also need energy (calories) for growth and development. This is particularly important in children up to the age of 5 years as this is a time of rapid growth in muscles and bone tissues and in the development of the brain.

Energy is measured in kilocalories (kcals), which is a metric term for calories. It can also be expressed in kiloJoules (kJ). 1kcal equals approximately 4.2kJ.

The importance of physical activity for the under-5s

The energy we need every day is determined both by a basic level of requirement to keep our bodies functioning (called the Basal Metabolic Rate or BMR) and by the amount of physical activity that we do (for example moving around, walking, or exercising). People who are inactive have lower energy needs and will eat less food to maintain their body weight. It becomes much harder to get all the nutrients needed for good health if less food is eaten.

Physical activity is essential for optimal growth and development in children. It is generally agreed that children now are less active than those in previous generations. This has been caused by a number of factors including, for example, the time spent watching television, with recent evidence suggesting that among 3-4 year olds TV viewing is positively associated with higher body weight: those spending longer periods of time watching TV tend to have a higher body weight.[4] A study of children in Glasgow suggests that children are developing sedentary lifestyles from a very early age, with 3 year olds and 5 year olds spending 79% and 76% of their time in sedentary behaviours respectively.[5] The Health Survey for England (2002)[6] and the Scottish Health Survey (2003)[7] suggest that about a third of under-5s do not take part in 60 minutes of moderate activity every day. Restrictions on children being able to walk to school or play freely outside, for safety reasons, contribute to this.[8]

How much energy do children need? Where do they get their energy (calories) from?

The energy needs of each individual are different, and recommendations for a healthy diet are often expressed as what proportion of energy should come from fat and carbohydrate (see *Fat* on the next page and *Carbohydrates* on page 22). The average amount of energy that a group of children of different ages from 1 year up to 4 years are likely to need are summarised below. (These are average figures for boys and girls: a more detailed breakdown of energy requirements by age and gender is given in Appendix 3.)

Age	Average energy requirements in kcals (calories) per day[1]
1 year	935kcals
2 years	1,160kcals
3 years	1,430kcals
4 years	1,530kcals

The nutrients fat, carbohydrate and protein all provide the body with calories. (For more about these nutrients see pages 21-24.) At present, under-5s in the UK get most of their energy from carbohydrates (about 51%) and fats (about 36%), with protein providing about 13%.[2]

The proportion of energy that under-5s currently get from carbohydrate and fat meets the recommendations. However, more of the energy from carbohydrates should be provided by cereal foods, vegetables and potatoes, and less from confectionery and soft drinks as these foods are high in sugar but provide few other nutrients.

It is important to note that children do not need sugar for energy. (For more information about sugar and other carbohydrates, see pages 22-23.)

The increase in childhood obesity in the UK has been well documented and approximately 30% of boys and 28% of girls aged 2-10 years are overweight or obese.[3] Obesity in children is difficult to treat as care must be taken to maintain growth and development. Overweight children should be encouraged to increase their activity. More information on physical activity can be found opposite and on page 46.

Fat

Fat in the diet

Fat provides the most concentrated form of energy in the diet.

There are basically two types of fat: **saturated fats**, which are mainly from animal sources; and **unsaturated fats**, which are found mainly in plants and fish. The unsaturated fats include a group called polyunsaturated fats.

Some fat in the diet is essential and the developing child has a particular need for what are known as 'essential fatty acids'. These are important for healthy development. Breast milk is relatively high in essential fatty acids to reflect this need. Fat in foods also provides some of the fat-soluble vitamins – vitamins A, D and E (see page 26).

How much fat should there be in children's diets? Are children getting too much?

Healthy eating recommendations for people aged over 5 are that total fat should provide no more than 35% of total food energy and that saturated fat should provide no more than 11% of food energy.[1] Between infancy and 5 years there is an expectation that the proportion of energy derived from fat will fall from 50% (as supplied by breastfeeding) to 35% (as recommended for adults).

There is discussion about whether the recommendations for the proportion of fat in the diet intended for everyone over 5 years of age (which are designed to reduce heart disease in the population) should also be applied to children under 5. The prevailing view is one of caution because there is concern that very low fat intakes may have an adverse impact on children's growth and development. There is also concern that children – who require a relatively nutrient-dense diet – may not get enough energy and nutrients if they are given low-fat foods. For example, it is recommended that children under the age of 2 years are given whole milk and that skimmed milk is not given before 5 years of age.[9] The term 'muesli belt malnutrition' was coined to describe children from relatively affluent households who failed to grow and develop normally when given diets inappropriately low in fat.

However, evidence from a large longitudinal study of children at 18 months suggests that there is no evidence that children who have fat intakes providing 30-35% of energy experience delayed growth and there is in fact evidence that children on higher fat diets (where 39-43% of energy is from fat) may have lower intakes of iron and vitamin C and lower iron status.[10] It was also reported that higher fat intakes were associated with higher total cholesterol levels among boys even at this young age, and this again may suggest that ensuring fat intakes are moderate among under-5s may be beneficial for future health.

Children between the ages of 1 and 4 years in Britain currently appear to get about 35% of their energy from fat[2] and maintaining this level of total fat intake is to be encouraged as children get older.

The intake of saturated fat among those aged 1-4 years is about 16% of food energy.[2] Although this is higher than the 11% recommended for people aged 5 years and over, this is to be expected since milk consumption in this group is high: almost a third of the saturated fat in the diets of under-5s is provided by milk.

n-3 polyunsaturated fats (omega-3 fats)

Long chain n-3 polyunsaturated fatty acids (also known as omega-3 fats) are derived primarily from oil-rich fish. The importance of omega-3 fats has been established for brain development in babies prenatally (in the womb)[11] and probably in early postnatal life and these fats are thought to be beneficial for heart health in adults.[12] There is, however, insubstantial evidence that supplements of omega-3 fats are beneficial for health in children or that they improve learning or concentration. (See *Diet, behaviour and learning in children* on page 53.)

The most significant natural food source of omega-3 fats is oil-rich fish such as salmon, trout, sprats, herring, mackerel, sardines, pilchards and fresh tuna. (Other n-3 polyunsaturated fats can be found in oils such as rapeseed oil and soya oil; walnuts and almonds; pumpkin seeds; organic milk; and green leafy vegetables such as broccoli and spinach. However, there is no evidence that these n-3 polyunsaturated fatty acids protect against heart disease.)

Carbohydrates

CARBOHYDRATES

STARCH

Starch is the main component of cereals, pulses, grains and root vegetables.

SUGARS

Intrinsic sugars

Milk sugars

Non-milk extrinsic sugars (NME sugars)

These sugars are found naturally in foods such as vegetables, fruits and milk.

This includes table sugar, sugar added to recipes, and sugars in soft drinks.

Carbohydrates is the term used to describe both **starch** and **sugars** in foods. Carbohydrates provide energy.

Starch is the major component of cereals, pulses, grains and root vegetables. Most people can visualise starchy foods when they think of flour and potato.

The term '**sugars**' is often assumed to describe something white and granular found in sugar bowls, but in fact the sugars found in foods can be quite variable. In order to clarify the roles of different sugars in health, the sugars in foods have been distinguished as: intrinsic sugars, milk sugars and non-milk extrinsic sugars (or NME sugars). Intrinsic sugars and milk sugars are the sugars found naturally in foods such as milk, vegetables and fruits. NME sugars include table sugar, sugar added to recipes, and honey. NME sugars are also found in foods such as confectionery, cakes, biscuits, sugary breakfast cereals, soft drinks and fruit juices.

It is recommended that, for the population as a whole, carbohydrates should provide about 50% of total food energy, and that most of this should come from starch, intrinsic sugars, and sugars found naturally in milk, and that 11% or less energy should be provided by sugars which have been primarily added to other foods.[1] Children do not need 'sugars' for energy. They can get all the energy they need from other carbohydrate foods. Although the current recommendations for intakes of sugars were designed for everyone over the age of 5, there is no evidence to suggest that children under 5 require diets that are higher in non-milk extrinsic sugars. Recent advice in Scotland recommends that non-milk extrinsic sugars

provide no more than 11% of food energy for children aged 1-5 years[13] and the Caroline Walker Trust supports this recommendation.

Starch, intrinsic sugars and milk sugars

How much do children need? Are they getting enough?

It is currently recommended that starch, intrinsic sugars and milk sugars together should provide about 40% of energy to the diet by the age of 5 years.[1] Starch, intrinsic sugars and milk sugars currently provide about 32% of all energy in the diets of 1-4 year olds in Britain, and 10% of this is provided by milk sugars.[2] As milk intakes decline and appetites increase it is recommended that foods such as bread, potatoes, pasta and rice replace the energy no longer provided by milk. Starchy foods such as these fill children up, are a good source of energy and can also provide important nutrients such as fibre and some of the B vitamins.

Younger children who have smaller appetites may find starchy foods very filling, and a balance is required between the energy provided by starchy foods and that from other foods such as, for example, meat and milk (and products containing meat or milk) which may provide energy with less bulk.

Sources of starch and intrinsic and milk sugars

Sources of starch

Sources of starch include bread, rice, chapatis, pasta, couscous, breakfast cereals, potatoes, yams and plantains. Whole grain cereals are a valuable source of fibre (see page 25) but can be bulky and should be introduced gradually to the diets of under-5s.

Sources of intrinsic and milk sugars

Sources of intrinsic and milk sugars include fruits (but not fruit juices – see below) and vegetables and milk.

Non-milk extrinsic sugars (NME sugars)

What are non-milk extrinsic sugars?

In the past, sugars were often referred to as 'added sugars' and 'natural sugars' – terms which many people found confusing. The Government's advisory panel COMA (Committee on Medical Aspects of Food and Nutrition Policy) defined different sugars in the diet more precisely depending on their effects on health. 'Non-milk extrinsic sugars' – or NME sugars – are those which have been extracted from a root, stem or fruit of a plant and are no longer incorporated into the cellular structure of food. NME sugars therefore include table sugar, sugar added to recipes, and sugars found in soft drinks and fruit juices. Honey is also included in this group.

The development of tooth decay is positively related to the amount and particularly the frequency of NME sugars in the diet.[14] This is most marked when sugar is eaten both at and between meals.

Sources of NME sugars

Sources of NME sugars include soft drinks, fruit juice, sweets, chocolate, cakes, biscuits, sugary breakfast cereals, table sugar and honey.

How much are children getting? Are they getting too much?

The recommendation to reduce the energy in the diet provided by NME sugars is primarily to prevent tooth decay.[1] The other concern is that foods high in NME sugars often provide calories but few other nutrients. This is particularly true for drinks such as squashes and fizzy drinks, sweets, and sugar added to drinks and cereals. Children need a relatively nutrient-dense diet. If a large proportion of the foods and drinks they consume are high in NME sugars, it may be difficult for under-5s to obtain all the nutrients they need each day.

The intakes of NME sugars among pre-school children in Britain are currently significantly higher than recommended. According to a national survey, children aged between 1 and 4 years in Britain obtain about 20% of their energy from NME sugars,[2] which is about twice the current recommendation. (The contribution of NME sugars to the diet should be no more than 11% of total food energy.) About 10% of the children in this survey were getting a third or more of their energy from NME sugars alone.

It is important to protect the first (milk) teeth of pre-school children so that these teeth stay in position to allow for the normal development of the permanent teeth. Pre-school children are considered at high risk for the development of tooth decay.[9]

When intakes of NME sugars are compared with dental health it has been shown that the consumption of sugary drinks at bedtime and frequent consumption of sugar confectionery and non-diet soft drinks are related to the amount of tooth decay.[15] For example, 40% of 3-4 year olds who had sugar confectionery most days, or more often, had experience of tooth decay, compared with 22% of those who had sugar confectionery less frequently.

It has also been reported that decay is more likely to affect pre-school children who are given first weaning foods containing sugar, those still drinking from a bottle at 2 years of age, and those who are given sweetened comforters (most commonly a sweet drink in a bottle or, less frequently, a dummy dipped in honey or jam).[16] It is therefore important not only to reduce the amount of NME sugars but also to reduce the frequency and the amount of contact that sugary foods and drinks have with the teeth.

The main sources of NME sugars among the under-5s are soft drinks (which contribute about a third of NME sugars), cereals and cereal products, and confectionery (which contribute about a quarter of NME sugars each) and table sugar itself which contributes about 5%.[2] Reducing the intake of soft drinks would have a major impact on the amount of NME sugars in many children's diets.

For more information about drinks for the under-5s and about dental health and practical ways to reduce tooth decay in the under-5s, see page 50.

Protein

Why children need protein

Protein is needed for growth and the maintenance and repair of body tissues and to make the enzymes that control many body functions.

How much protein do children need? Are they getting enough?

Protein needs are proportionally higher for children than for adults but most children in Britain have more than adequate intakes of protein. For example, children aged between 1 and 4 have an average intake of 36.4g protein a day and those aged 4-4$\frac{1}{2}$ years an average intake of 39.4g a day.[2] These figures, which are typical for Western diets, are above the Reference Nutrient Intakes for protein of 14.5g a day for 1-3 year olds and 19.7g a day for 4-6 year olds.[1] (The Reference Nutrient Intake is the amount of a nutrient which is likely to meet the requirements of most children – see opposite.)

Protein is available from both animal and vegetable foods, so vegetarian children can get enough protein as long as they get a good variety of foods every day. For more information on vegetarian diets see page 51.

Sources of protein

Sources of protein include: milk, meat, poultry, fish, eggs, cheese, tofu, pulses such as peas, beans and lentils, and cereal foods such as bread, rice and pasta.

In Britain, children under 5 get about a third of their protein from milk and milk products, a quarter from cereals and cereal products, and another quarter from meat and meat products.[2]

What is a Reference Nutrient Intake?

The Reference Nutrient Intake (RNI) is the amount of a nutrient that is likely to meet the requirements of nearly everybody in a group. If people get more than this amount, they will almost certainly be getting enough. Reference Nutrient Intakes have been set for many nutrients including protein, B vitamins (thiamin, riboflavin and niacin), folate, vitamins C and A, calcium, iron and zinc.

Fibre

Why children need fibre

Fibre (or NSP – non-starch polysaccharides) represents those parts of cereal and vegetable foods which are not broken down in the small intestine and which are particularly important to prevent constipation and other bowel disorders. It is also suggested that some components of NSP are important for lowering blood cholesterol levels.

How much do children need? Are they getting enough?

There is little evidence for the effects of dietary fibre in young children and no recommendation for NSP intake is made. It would seem sensible that children should have proportionally lower intakes compared to adults, for whom the recommendation is 18g a day. It has been reported that children aged $1^1/_2$-$4^1/_2$ years have an average intake of 6.1g fibre a day.[2]

Little information is available on normal bowel movements in pre-school children or its relation to fibre intake. One study reported that children with a higher average daily intake of fibre are more likely to have more frequent bowel movements.[2]

Constipation in children can be related to poor intakes of fibre and fluid, emotional disturbances and changes in routine.[17] Constipation may be alleviated by a modest increase in fibre-rich food (particularly fortified high-fibre breakfast cereals, wholemeal bread and fruit and vegetables). It is very important that adequate fluids are drunk if fibre intakes are increased or if children appear constipated. Raw bran should never be given to the under-5s as it can cause bloating, wind and loss of appetite and affect the absorption of other important nutrients. If constipation becomes troublesome, medical advice should be sought.

The fears that high-fibre diets in under-5s will lead to growth-faltering and mineral imbalance in the developed world are not well supported by research studies[18] and it is suggested that, with rising childhood obesity, increases in fibre may help to reduce energy intake. However, those children under 2 who are fussy eaters should not be given fibre-rich foods at the expense of energy-rich foods which they require for adequate growth.

Sources of fibre

Sources of fibre include wholemeal bread, whole grain breakfast cereals, pulses (peas, beans and lentils), and fresh and dried fruit and vegetables. These foods provide useful sources of other nutrients too.

For more information on sources of fibre, see page 80.

Toddler diarrhoea

Frequent loose stools containing recognisable food matter (such as fruit and vegetable skins, or sweetcorn) is a common problem in some children who are otherwise healthy. While this is generally harmless and will improve on its own as the child gets older, excessive fluid intake from fruit squashes and fruit juices should be discouraged. Clear apple juice contains large quantities of non-absorbable sugars which can make the condition worse.[19] Encouraging a normal diet which contains foods from all the food groups should be encouraged as some parents may needlessly restrict some food items because they believe that they exacerbate the diarrhoea.

Prebiotics and probiotics

'Oligosaccharides' are a component of dietary fibre that have been shown to have 'prebiotic effects'. This means that they encourage the growth of lactic acid bacteria, in particular bifidobacteria. These bacteria are similar to those included in foods and drinks which contain probiotics. It has been suggested that these bacteria can have a beneficial effect on reducing the incidence of diarrhoea and some allergies (such as eczema) in young children but there have been insufficient studies to establish whether there is any benefit in taking supplements of these foods. Including good natural sources of oligosaccharides such as pulses, fruits and whole grains in the diet will promote good gut health in young children.

Vitamins

Vitamins are often divided into two groups: those that are water-soluble and those that are fat-soluble. Some vitamins are found predominantly or only in animal foods – for example vitamin D and vitamin B_{12}. Others are found predominantly or only in foods from vegetable origin, for example vitamin C.

The fat-soluble vitamins (A, D, E and K) are stored in the body and high doses of vitamins A and D should not be given.

Water-soluble vitamins (thiamin, riboflavin, niacin, vitamin B_6, vitamin B_{12}, folate and vitamin C) are not stored in the body and, because they are water-soluble, they can leach out into cooking water and are also more likely to be destroyed if foods containing them are over-cooked or exposed to the air for long periods.

Reference Nutrient Intakes for the under-5s have been set for all vitamins except vitamin E and vitamin K. Not enough information is available at present to set a Reference Nutrient Intake for these vitamins.

It is important for children to get enough of each vitamin. However, having too much does not bring any benefit and may be harmful.

Fat-soluble vitamins

Vitamin A
Vitamin D
Vitamin E
Vitamin K

These are stored in the body. Vitamin A in food can be destroyed by heat or by oxidation if left exposed to the air.

Water-soluble vitamins

B vitamins: thiamin, riboflavin, niacin
Vitamin B_6
Vitamin B_{12}
Folate
Vitamin C

These are not stored in the body. They are water-soluble, so they are more likely to be destroyed by heat or by oxidation if left exposed to the air.

Vitamin A (also known as retinol equivalents)

Why children need vitamin A

Vitamin A comes in two forms: retinol, which is only found in animal foods; and carotene, the yellow or orange pigment found in fruit and vegetables (both those coloured yellow or orange and in many green ones where the orange colour is masked by chlorophyll pigment). Carotene can be converted into retinol by the body. It takes 6 units of carotene to make 1 unit of retinol.

Vitamin A is often thought of as the 'anti-infection' vitamin as it plays an important role in maintaining the immune system. It is also essential for growth, which is why children have a relatively higher requirement for vitamin A than adults. Vitamin A is also associated with good vision in dim light as retinol is essential for the substance in the eye which allows night vision.

Experts now believe that carotene has a much wider role than just as a means to produce vitamin A. It may protect the body from internal damage which could lead eventually to heart disease or the development of cancer.

How much do children need? Are they getting enough?

Vitamin A is the most difficult vitamin to get right in the diets of children, as both deficiency and excess can be a problem. Children aged 1-3 years have a Reference Nutrient Intake (RNI) for vitamin A of 400 micrograms a day and those aged 4-6 years of 500 micrograms a day[1] (see Appendix 3).

A national survey of children aged $1^1/_2$-$4^1/_2$ years showed that almost half of all children had intakes below the Reference Nutrient Intake and 8% of children had very low intakes.[2] This may be due to the fact that only a limited number of foods are sources of vitamin A and many children are low consumers of vegetables. For this reason, vitamin drops containing vitamin A are recommended for all under-5s. However, it is important not to give more vitamin drops than recommended because very high intakes of vitamin A can be dangerous. They can cause liver and bone damage, hair loss, double vision, vomiting and headaches.

It is recommended that regular intakes from food sources and vitamin drops should not exceed 900 micrograms a day among infants, 1,800 micrograms a day among 1-3 year olds and 3,000 micrograms a day among 4-6 year olds.[1] A normal diet and appropriate use of vitamin drops (5 drops a day) should give no cause for concern.

For information on vitamin drops see the next page.

Sources of vitamin A

Retinol

Few foods provide retinol naturally. Butter contains retinol as does cheese and to a lesser extent eggs. Margarine is fortified with vitamin A by law, and other fat spreads may also be fortified in this way. It is worth checking the label of other fat spreads to see if they are fortified. Milk and milk products usually provide about a third of daily vitamin A intakes in young children.

Liver and liver pâté can contain very high levels of vitamin A since animals store vitamin A in their livers. It is recommended that these foods are given to children no more than once a week.[20]

Carotene

Carrots are the best source of carotene but other orange foods such as sweet potatoes, mango, melon and apricots (dried or fresh) as well as green leafy vegetables (eg. spinach, watercress, broccoli), tomatoes and red peppers are also good sources.

For more information on sources of vitamin A, see Appendix 2.

Vitamins (continued)

Vitamin D

Why children need vitamin D

Vitamin D is needed for healthy bones and teeth. Prolonged deficiency of vitamin D in children results in rickets, the main signs of which are skeletal malformation (eg. bowed legs) with bone pain or tenderness and muscle weakness. A child with vitamin D deficiency is usually miserable and lethargic.

How much do children need? Are they getting enough?

The main source of vitamin D is by exposure of the skin to ultraviolet (UV) radiation in summer sunlight. Infants and children aged between 6 months and 3 years are particularly vulnerable to vitamin D depletion because of their rapid bone growth and the limited exposure some may have to UV radiation. Vitamin D is present in a limited number of foods and it is difficult for young children to obtain satisfactory vitamin D intakes from diet alone.

After the age of 3 years, people are generally able to maintain satisfactory vitamin D status from sunlight if they spend sufficient time outside between April and September. The recommendation for infants and children aged between 7 months and 3 years is 7 micrograms of vitamin D a day.[1] It is recommended however that children up to 5 years of age receive supplementary vitamin D in vitamin drops.[9] (See box below.)

There are concerns about the link between the exposure of the skin to UV radiation and subsequent skin cancer. It is recommended that children should be protected from the sun by using shade, wearing a sunhat and applying a high factor sunscreen on bare skin.[21] Using sunblocks on young children makes the use of vitamin D supplements especially important.

Under-5s of Asian origin are more likely to have lower vitamin D status, and a resurgence of rickets has been reported in many cities in the UK.[22] This may be due to a number of factors including diet, a more limited exposure to the sun and wearing more clothing when outside. Vitamin drops are particularly important for these children.

It is important not to exceed the recommended dose. High doses of vitamin D can be dangerous and the gap between the requirement and the toxic dose is not large. As little as five times the recommended intake taken regularly is associated with symptoms of vitamin D toxicity.

Sources of vitamin D

Very few foods are good sources of vitamin D. Oily fish such as tuna, salmon and pilchards provide vitamin D as do foods fortified by manufacturers such as margarine, many fat spreads and breakfast cereals. Infant formula also contains vitamin D. The main dietary sources of vitamin D among those aged $1^1/_2$-$4^1/_2$ years are fat spreads and fortified breakfast cereals.[2]

For more information on sources of vitamin D, see Appendix 2.

Vitamin drops

The Department of Health recommends that all children up to the age of 5 receive vitamin supplements (vitamin drops) containing vitamins A, C and D. These vitamins are currently free to children up to 5 years old in low-income families (families in receipt of Income Support, income-based Jobseeker's Allowance or Child Tax Credit [but not Working Tax Credit] with an income below a certain amount [£14,155 a year in 2006/7]), through the Welfare Food Scheme. This scheme is being replaced in phases and will include distribution of the new Healthy Start children's vitamin drops (see www.healthystart.nhs.uk). Parents can get more information on vitamin drops from their health visitor or GP.

B vitamins: thiamin, riboflavin and niacin

Why children need the B vitamins thiamin, riboflavin and niacin

B vitamins are particularly important for the brain and nervous system. The body also needs these B vitamins – thiamin, riboflavin and niacin – to be able to use the energy (calories) in food.

How much do children need? Are they getting enough?

Average intakes of these vitamins are higher than the Reference Nutrient Intakes, with few children aged 1$\frac{1}{2}$-4$\frac{1}{2}$ years having intakes below those amounts.[2] However, those children with low intakes need particular attention.

A varied diet which provides sufficient energy and protein will usually provide enough of these vitamins at the same time.

Sources of thiamin and niacin

Sources of thiamin and niacin include: bread and other foods made with flour, breakfast cereals, pork (including bacon and ham), fish, yeast extract (eg. marmite) and potatoes.

Sources of riboflavin

Sources of riboflavin include: milk and milk products such as yoghurt; poultry; meat; oily fish (such as tuna, salmon or sardines); and eggs. Milk and milk products provide about 50% of the daily riboflavin intakes for children aged 1$\frac{1}{2}$-4$\frac{1}{2}$ in Britain.[2]

For more information on sources of thiamin, riboflavin and niacin, see Appendix 2.

Folate

Why children need folate

Folates are a group of compounds, found in foods, which collectively are known as 'folate' or 'folic acid'.

Folate is an essential vitamin for many vital metabolic processes, and deficiency can lead to a particular type of anaemia known as megaloblastic anaemia.

How much do children need? Are they getting enough?

Accurate dietary assessment of folate is difficult, but intakes among children aged 1$\frac{1}{2}$-4$\frac{1}{2}$ years appear to be adequate.[2]

Children obtain over a third of their folate from cereal products, particularly breakfast cereals, about a fifth from vegetables, potatoes and snacks, and almost a fifth from milk and milk products.[2]

Sources of folate

Sources of folate include green leafy vegetables and salads, oranges and other citrus fruits, liver* and yeast extract as well as foods which have been fortified including breakfast cereals and some breads.

Folate is partly destroyed by prolonged heating, for example by overcooking food or by heating it and keeping it for long periods.

For more information on sources of folate, see Appendix 2.

---

* Liver, including liver pâté, is very rich in vitamin A which can be harmful in large amounts (see page 27). It is recommended that these foods are given to children no more than once a week.[20]

Vitamins (continued)

Vitamin B6

Why children need vitamin B6

Vitamin B6 is the name given to a whole group of substances that are commonly found in both animal and vegetable foods and which are involved in a number of body processes involving amino acids (the protein building blocks).

How much do children need? Are they getting enough?

Deficiency is rare. If children have a varied diet they are unlikely to be deficient in vitamin B6.

Sources of vitamin B6

Good sources of vitamin B6 include liver*, red meat, poultry, oily fish, bananas, potatoes, whole grain cereals and nuts.

Vitamin B12

Why children need vitamin B12

Vitamin B12 interacts with folate and vitamin B6. Together these vitamins help the body to build up its own protein, especially for nervous tissue and red blood cells.

How much do children need? Are they getting enough?

Vitamin B12 is found almost exclusively in animal products.

Deficiency of this vitamin in under-5s is virtually unknown except when animal products are very strictly excluded from the diet (for example, vegan diets and more restrictive diets).

Sources of vitamin B12

All foods of animal origin contain vitamin B12 – for example meat, fish and milk. Some other foods are fortified with vitamin B12, such as fortified breakfast cereals and some yeast extracts.

* Liver, including liver pâté, is very rich in vitamin A which can be harmful in large amounts (see page 27). It is recommended that these foods are given to children no more than once a week.[20]

Vitamin C

Why children need vitamin C

Vitamin C has an important role in preventing disease and maintaining good health. The body needs vitamin C to produce and maintain collagen, the foundation material for bones, teeth, skin and tendons. It is also important in wound healing. It is suggested that vitamin C has a role as an antioxidant vitamin in preventing damage to cells and tissues. Vitamin C may also assist the absorption of iron in the diet if both nutrients are present in the same meal.

How much do children need? Are they getting enough?

The Reference Nutrient Intake for children over 1 year for vitamin C is 30mg a day.[1] In a national study of children aged $1^1/_2$-$4^1/_2$ years,[2] 38% of children had intakes of vitamin C below the Reference Nutrient Intake.

Lower intakes of vitamin C are reported in children of lower socioeconomic status and in children living in Scotland. These lower intakes are attributable to the lower intakes of fruit and vegetables, which are the major source of vitamin C.

Children currently obtain 50% of their vitamin C from soft drinks and fruit juice, with soft drinks (such as blackcurrant drinks) contributing 30% of vitamin C. Vegetables and potatoes contributed 19% of total vitamin C intake, 13% of which was from potatoes and savoury snacks. Fruit contributed only 15% of total daily vitamin C.

The under-5s in the UK currently eat too little fruit and vegetables and the variety is limited. The national study mentioned above found that peas and carrots are the vegetables most commonly eaten by the under-5s. Leafy green vegetables were eaten by less than 39% of children, and raw vegetables and salad were eaten by less than a quarter of children during the 4-day study period. The average intake of all vegetable foods (excluding baked beans and potatoes) reported among children aged $1^1/_2$-$4^1/_2$ years was 27g a day.[2] In the same survey fruit intake averaged 50g a day, two-thirds of which was apples and bananas. The recommendation to offer fruit and vegetables at

5 A DAY

Children and adults are advised to eat at least five portions of fruit and vegetables every day. This should preferably include two portions of fruit (one can be fruit juice) and three portions of vegetables. (Dark green and orange vegetables are particularly encouraged.)

Children under 5 are encouraged to have five different tastes of fruit and vegetables every day. This will encourage them to accept a wider variety of these foods and eat more fruit and vegetables as they get older and their appetite increases.

Children under 5 in child care should have fruits and vegetables offered as part of all their main meals. Snacks provide an opportunity for children to try new types of fruits and vegetables. Examples of good snacks can be found on pages 45 and 55.

Some tinned and dried fruits contain added sugar and some tinned vegetables and purchased vegetable dishes may also be high in salt. Carers should look for fruit and vegetable products which do not have salt and sugar added, but fresh, frozen, dried and tinned varieties can be included in the diet.

Fruit juice (100% juice) can be included as a portion of fruit, but fruit juices contain sugar and acid that can damage teeth and should be served diluted, and preferably with meals. For more information about fruit juices and other drinks, see page 49.

each meal and with some snacks each day (see *5 A DAY* above) would ensure adequate vitamin C (and folate) intakes.

It is important that fruit and vegetables are eaten every day as vitamin C cannot be stored in the body.

Sources of vitamin C

Sources of vitamin C include: fruit and fruit juices, potatoes (including chips) and other vegetables. Citrus fruits such as oranges are particularly good sources as are red and green peppers, spring greens, blackcurrants and strawberries. Some drinks are also fortified with vitamin C (see *Drinks for the under-5s* on page 47).

For more information on sources of vitamin C, see Appendix 2.

Minerals

There are a number of minerals in the diet including iron, calcium, zinc, copper, iodine, magnesium, phosphorus, potassium and selenium.[1] Reference Nutrient Intakes have been set for all these minerals. Low intakes of iron and zinc have been reported in the diets of the under-5s. Sodium (which is found in salt) is also discussed here as there are recommendations to reduce the amount of sodium in the diet.

Iron

Why children need iron

Iron is essential for the function of several body systems and particularly as part of the pigment in red blood cells called haemoglobin, which carries oxygen. A deficiency in iron can cause anaemia. Iron deficiency means that the blood transports less oxygen for the body's needs and so limits the person's ability to be physically active. Children with iron deficiency will be pale and tired and their general health, resistance to infection, appetite and vitality will be impaired.[23] Sometimes there are no apparent symptoms and iron deficiency may be undetected. Prevention of iron deficiency is important because, apart from these immediate effects, it is suggested that iron deficiency in children has an immediate and longer term impact on intellectual performance and behaviour.[24, 25]

How much iron do children need? Are they getting enough?

The current Reference Nutrient Intakes for iron are:
- 6.9mg a day for children aged 1-3 years, and
- 6.1mg a day for children aged 4-6 years.

The higher requirement for the younger age group reflects their increased needs during this period of rapid growth and development.

Deficiency of iron is common in most countries, especially among children aged 1-3 years. It can be assessed either by measuring the amount of iron in the diet, or by measuring the amount of iron being carried in the blood (haemoglobin).

Eighty-four per cent of children in Britain have intakes below the Reference Nutrient Intake for iron and almost one in five have very low intakes.[2]

Preventing iron deficiency: what can help?

- Where an infant is not being breastfed, infant formula (which contains added iron) should be used rather than cow's milk until the age of 12 months. It has been suggested that, if there are concerns about the adequacy of iron in a child's diet, it might be wise to extend the use of these milks into toddlerhood.[9] These milks should be used as part of a balanced weaning diet. Where an infant is being breastfed it is important to provide a variety of weaning foods from 6 months.

- Overdependence on milk puts toddlers at risk of iron deficiency, particularly where children do not have good intakes of foods known to enhance iron status, such as meat or fruit. Offering milk drinks after meals rather than during meals will help to ensure that children eat a variety of foods.

- For older children, diets that provide plenty of iron have lots of meat*, poultry, fish and fruits and vegetables. Children who do not eat meat or fish require a diet of variety containing foods such as cereal foods, pulses, finely ground nuts, vegetables and fruit. For more information about vegetarian diets, see page 51.

- Although iron from plant foods is not absorbed by the body as well as iron from animal sources, there are ways of increasing the amount absorbed:

  - Foods with lots of vitamin C may help the body absorb iron if eaten at the same time. Fruit and fruit juices, tomatoes and some green vegetables are good sources of vitamin C. Having a fruit juice along with an iron-fortified breakfast cereal, for example, will provide a good start to the day.

  - Meat* also helps the absorption of iron from vegetable foods.

- Some foods can hinder the absorption of non-haem iron from foods. For example, tannic acid in tea and coffee can reduce the amount of iron absorbed. It is advisable not to give these drinks to children. If given at breakfast, for example, they would hinder the absorption of the iron in a fortified breakfast cereal. If tea or coffee is given it should be very weak, and be served without sugar, and should only be given between meals.

* **Meat, meat products and meat dishes**
Because of food scares in the past, some parents may be concerned about giving meat to children. However, meat is a very important source not only of iron but also of zinc, another essential nutrient.

Children aged $1^1/2$-$4^1/2$ years have been reported to consume on average about 5.5mg of iron a day.[2]

Iron deficiency is frequently reported in studies of the under-5s and the national survey of children aged $1^1/2$-$4^1/2$ years found that 1 in 12 children overall, and 1 in 8 of those aged $1^1/2$-$2^1/2$ had low haemoglobin levels in their blood.[2] For children in poorer areas it is estimated that 1 in 6 white children between the ages of 1 and 2 years are iron-deficient.[26] The incidence of iron deficiency is known to be greater among children from ethnic minority groups and a national study found that up to one-third of toddlers from three different Asian groups living in the UK had iron deficiency.[27]

Another measure of iron status is to measure the amount of iron stores in the blood (measured as serum ferritin). Among children aged $1^1/2$-$4^1/2$ years, 1 in 5 children had low iron stores, and 1 in 20 children had very low iron stores, measured as low serum ferritin.[2]

Causes of iron deficiency

The risk of iron deficiency among young children is highest among those under 3 years, as this is a time of rapid growth. During this period children need to double the iron stores in their body. Babies born prematurely have lower stores of iron at birth and may also experience rapid catch-up growth, which demands more iron. These factors make them more vulnerable to iron deficiency.

Iron deficiency is more often associated with prolonged milk feeding (for example where a variety of foods are not introduced from 6 months of age and where milk continues to be the main food source during the first years of life) or a weaning diet which contains little iron. Overdependence on milk where this displaces iron-rich or iron-enhancing foods is significantly related to low iron status in pre-school children.[28] Asian children consuming more than 600-700ml of cow's milk daily have been shown to be at high risk of iron deficiency.[2] It has been suggested that the lack of manufactured meat-based weaning foods suitable for those who require halal foods may contribute to low iron intakes among infants of Asian origin.[29] Vegetarian and vegan children are also at greater risk of iron deficiency although this can be avoided and research has shown that adequate iron status is achievable with vegetarian diets.[30] Some foods and drinks inhibit the absorption of iron and may therefore contribute to iron deficiency. For example,

tea drinking has been associated with poorer iron status among pre-school children.[31]

Haem iron from animal sources is absorbed more easily into the body than non-haem iron from vegetable sources. However, only a small proportion of the iron consumed by under-5s – just over 5% – is haem iron.[2] Children's low intakes of haem iron reflect their relatively low intakes of meat and meat products which are very important sources of iron. In a national survey of children, only half of the children ate beef, beef dishes, poultry or sausages during the four-day recording period, and less than 20% of children ate other meat and meat products during that period. The main sources of non-haem iron in the diets of children aged $1^1/2$-$4^1/2$ years were fortified cereals and cereal products, which accounted for half the total iron intake.[2]

Sources of iron

There are two forms of iron in foods:

- **haem iron**, which is found in foods of animal origin such as meat and meat products and oily fish, and
- **non-haem iron**, which is found in foods of plant origin such as cereals and vegetables.

Haem iron is found in foods of animal origin such as beef, lamb, chicken and turkey, liver* and kidney, and in some fish such as sardines and tuna. Haem iron is absorbed into the body more easily than non-haem iron.

Non-haem iron is found in foods of plant origin including cereal foods like bread, pulses such as peas, beans and lentils, dried fruits and green vegetables. It is also found in fortified breakfast cereals. The absorption of non-haem iron may be enhanced if foods or drinks rich in vitamin C are consumed at the same time.

The use of iron-fortified infant formula or breast milk during the first year of life is recommended and there is also some evidence that continuing formula milk into the second year of life reduces iron deficiency.[32] However, formula milks are expensive and encouraging a varied diet will have longer term benefits.

For more information on sources of iron, see Appendix 2.

---

* Liver, including liver pâté, is very rich in vitamin A which can be harmful in large amounts (see page 27). It is recommended that these foods are given to children no more than once a week.[20]

Minerals (continued)

Calcium

Why children need calcium

Calcium is required for building and maintaining bones, for the transmission of nerve impulses and muscle actions and for many other body functions.

How much do children need? Are they getting enough?

The current Reference Nutrient Intakes for calcium intake among children are:

- 350mg a day for 1-3 year olds, and
- 450mg a day for 4-6 year olds.[1]

The majority of children under 5 have adequate calcium intakes, with average intakes of about 600mg a day. About 50% of the calcium in the diets of under-5s comes from milk.[2] For more information about milk drinking in the under-5s see page 47.

It is important to ensure that children who do not have milk or dairy products have sufficient calcium, for example in a soya drink which has been fortified with calcium, or from tinned fish mashed with the bones. For more information about dairy-free diets, see page 52.

Sources of calcium

Sources of calcium include: milk, soya drink fortified with calcium, yoghurt, cheese, cheese spread, bread, tinned fish (eaten with the bones), tofu, egg yolk, pulses such as beans, lentils and chick peas, green leafy vegetables and ground almonds.

For more information on sources of calcium, see Appendix 2.

Zinc

Why children need zinc

Zinc plays a major role in the functioning of every organ in the body. It is needed for normal metabolism of protein, fat and carbohydrate and is associated with the hormone insulin which regulates the body's energy.

Zinc is also involved in the immune system, the utilisation of vitamin A, and in wound healing. Although it is known to have all those functions, more research is needed before the role of zinc can be defined more precisely.

How much do children need? Are they getting enough?

The Reference Nutrient Intakes for zinc are:

- 5mg a day for children aged 1-3, and
- 6.5mg a day for children aged 4-6 years.[1]

Lower intakes of zinc than these among children are frequently reported. In a national study of 1½-4½ year olds, more than 70% of children had intakes below the Reference Nutrient Intakes. A large proportion of children had very low intakes: 14% of under-4s and 37% of 4-6 year olds.[2, 34]

A third of zinc in the diets of the under-5s is provided by milk and milk products, a quarter by cereals and cereal products, and a quarter from meat and meat products. The intake of zinc has been shown to go down relative to energy intake as children get older, and as the intake of milk declines.[2] An increase in the intake of meat and meat dishes will ensure a higher zinc intake. For those not eating meat, whole grain cereals and breakfast cereals, milk, milk products and eggs should be included regularly in the diet.

Sources of zinc

Sources of zinc include meat, eggs, milk, cheese, whole grain cereals, nuts and pulses.

Sodium

Sodium in the diet

Sodium is essential but too much can be potentially dangerous for young children. Their kidneys are not yet fully developed and cannot excrete excess amounts of sodium, which may accumulate and cause harm.

How much sodium do children need? Are they getting too much?

The main source of sodium in the diet is as salt (also called sodium chloride), added to manufactured foods and used in cooking and at the table. It is generally agreed that most people in Britain eat too much salt and there is evidence that this leads to raised blood pressure in later life.[33] Accustoming children to food which is salty early in life may encourage a lasting taste for salty foods. The population targets for average salt consumption are:[33]

- 1-3 year olds: no more than 2g salt (equivalent to about 800mg sodium) per day
- 4-6 year olds: no more than 3g salt (equivalent to about 1,200mg sodium) per day.

Little data are available on the salt intakes of infants and very young children but estimated average intakes based on dietary intakes of children aged $1^{1}/_{2}$- $4^{1}/_{2}$ years suggest that intakes are in the region of 1,300-1,500mg of sodium per day (equivalent to 3.3g-3.8g of salt).[2] It is estimated that 4-6 year olds have about 5g of salt a day.[34] Children who regularly eat snack foods such as crisps and other savoury snacks, processed meat (such as salami or ham), cheese and tinned foods such as beans or spaghetti in sauce, are probably getting far more salt than they need. Salt should not be added to the diet of the under-5s in cooking or at the table.

Sources of sodium

Children should not eat foods which are high in sodium too often. Foods high in sodium include: sauces, soups, bacon, ham, sausage, smoked cheese, smoked fish, crisps, salted snacks and some breakfast cereals. Take-away and fast foods such as pizzas, burgers and coated chicken products are also likely to be very high in salt. More information on sources of sodium in foods and dishes can be found in *Eating Well for Under-5s in Child Care: Training Materials* (see page 87).

Fresh meat and poultry and all fresh and frozen fruit and vegetables are low in sodium and are suitable for children, as are unprocessed breakfast cereals such as porridge.

Other minerals

A number of other minerals have a Reference Nutrient Intake and these are summarised briefly below.

Copper

Copper is an essential component of many substances which control body functions. Copper intakes have been found to be lower than the Reference Nutrient Intake among about a third of under-5s.[2] We do not yet know whether the health of those with low intakes is compromised. No tests are yet available to make this assessment. Copper is found in a wide variety of foods but is found particularly in vegetables, fish and liver*.

Iodine

Iodine helps to make thyroid hormones necessary for maintaining the metabolic rate, and in infants it is essential for the development of the nervous system. Iodine deficiency is now rare in the UK but is still common in many areas of the world, where infants born to mothers with severe iodine deficiency are likely to suffer mental retardation. Iodine is found in milk and fish in particular and intakes are generally in excess of requirements. Very high intakes can be toxic.

Magnesium

Magnesium is important for the development of the skeleton and for maintaining nerve and muscle function. The main sources of magnesium in the diet are cereals and green vegetables, with cereal foods providing about a third of daily magnesium intake.[2]

---

* Liver, including liver pâté, is very rich in vitamin A which can be harmful in large amounts (see page 27). It is recommended that these foods are given to children no more than once a week.[20]

Minerals (continued)

Phosphorus

About 80% of the phosphorus in the body is present in the bones and phosphorus, with calcium, provides rigidity to the skeleton. Phosphorus is found in all plant and animal cells and therefore children will get enough phosphorus as long as they eat a varied diet.

Potassium

Potassium helps to regulate body fluids and also has a role in nerve and muscle function. It is therefore important for children to have an adequate intake. A large range of foods contain potassium and an inadequate intake is unlikely if children have a varied diet. Potassium is particularly abundant in vegetables, potatoes, fruit and juices.

Selenium

Selenium is involved in the mechanism which protects the body from damage inside the individual cells due to oxidation. There is little evidence to suggest that low intakes of selenium are associated with ill health in the UK. Selenium is found mainly in cereals, meat and fish, with cereals contributing about half of selenium intake in the UK.

Examples of good sources of vitamins and minerals in foods can be found in Appendix 2. Details of the Dietary Reference Values for all nutrients for under-5s are given in Appendix 3.

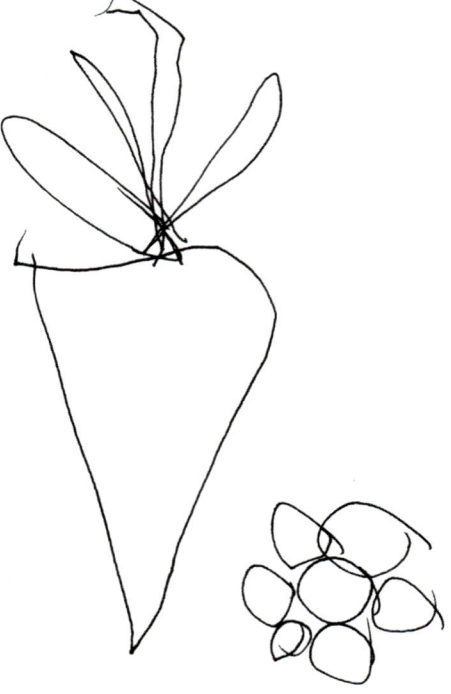

Carrot and a flower
Thomas, aged 4

References

1   Department of Health. 1991. *Dietary Reference Values for Food Energy and Nutrients for the United Kingdom. Report on Health and Social Subjects No. 41.* London: HMSO.

2   Gregory JR, Collins DL, Davies PSW, Hughes JM, Clarke PC. 1995. *National Diet and Nutrition Survey: Children Aged 1^1/$_2$ to 4^1/$_2$ Years. Volume 1: Report of the Diet and Nutrition Survey.* London: HMSO.

3   Department of Health. 2006. *Health Survey for England 2004.* Accessed from www.ic.nhs.uk/pubs/hsechildobesityupdate

4   Jago R, Baranowski T, Baranowski JC, Thompson D, Greaves KA. 2005. BMI from 3-6 years of age is predicted by TV viewing and physical activity, not diet. *International Journal of Obesity;* 29: 557-564.

5   Reilly JJ, Jackson DM, Montgomery C, Kelly LA, Slater C, Grant S, Paton JY. 2004. Total energy expenditure and physical activity in young Scottish children: mixed longitudinal study. *The Lancet;* 363: 211-212.

6   Sproston K, Primatesta P (eds.) 2003. *Health Survey for England 2002: The Health of Children and Young People.* London: TSO

7   Scottish Executive 2005. *The Scottish Health Survey: Volume 3 Children.* Edinburgh: Scottish Executive.

8   Wallace W. 1996. Food for thought. *Nursery World;* 96: 8-9.

9   Department of Health. 1994. *Weaning and the Weaning Diet. Report on Health and Social Subjects No. 45.* London: HMSO.

10   Rogers J, Emmett P and the ALSPAC Study Team. 2002. Fat content of the diet among pre-school children in Britain: relationship with food and nutrient intakes. *European Journal of Clinical Nutrition;* 56: 252-263.

11   Yehuda S, Rabinovitz S, Mostofsky DI. 1999. Essential fatty acids are mediators of brain biochemistry and cognitive functions. *Journal of Neuroscience Research;* 56: 565-570.

12   Department of Health. 1994. *Diet and Cardiovascular Disease.* London: HMSO.

13   Scottish Executive. 2006. *Nutritional Guidance for Early Years.* Edinburgh: Scottish Executive.

14   Department of Health. 1989. *Dietary Sugars and Human Disease. Report of the Committee on Medical Aspects of Food Policy.* London: HMSO.

15   Hinds K, Gregory J. 1995. *National Diet and Nutrition Survey: Children Aged 1^1/$_2$ to 4^1/$_2$ Years. Volume 2: Report of the Dental Survey.* London: HMSO.

16   Holt RD, Winter GB, Downer MC, Bellis MJ, Hay IS. 1996. Caries in pre-school children in Camden in 1993/94. *British Dental Journal;* 181: 405-411.

17   Burnett C, Wilkins G. 2002. Managing children with constipation. *Journal of Family Health Care;* 12: 127-132.

18   Edwards CA, Parrett AM. 2003. Dietary fibre in infancy and childhood. *Proceedings of the Nutrition Society;* 62: 17-23.

19   Hoekstra JH. 1998. Toddler diarrhoea: more a nutritional disorder than a disease. *Archives of Disease in Childhood;* 79; 2-5.

20   Scientific Advisory Committee on Nutrition. 2005. *Review of Dietary Advice on Vitamin A.* London: TSO.

21   Health Education Authority. 1999. *Sun Safety Guidelines for Schools.* Available through NICE at www.publichealth.nice.org.uk

22   Shaw NJ, Pal BR. 2002. Vitamin D deficiency in UK Asian families: activating a new concern. *Archives of Disease in Childhood,* 86: 147-149.

23   Oski FA. 1993. Iron deficiency in infancy and children. *New England Journal of Medicine;* 329: 190-193.

24   Walter T. 1993. Impact of iron deficiency on cognition in infancy and childhood. *European Journal of Clinical Nutrition;* 47: 307-316.

25   Lansdown R, Wharton BA. 1995. Iron and mental and motor behaviour in children. In: *Iron: Nutritional and Physiological Significance. The Report of The British Nutrition Foundation's Task Force.* London: Chapman and Hall: pages 61-74.

26   James J, Evans J, Male P, Pallister C, Hendrikz JK, Oakhill A. 1988. Iron deficiency in inner city pre-school children: development of a general practice screening programme in an inner city practice. *Journal of the Royal College of General Practitioners;* 38: 250-252.

27   Lawson MS, Thomas M, Hardiman A. 1998. Iron status of Asian children aged 2 years living in England. *Archives of Disease in Childhood;* 78: 420-426.

28   Thane CW, Walmsley CM, Bates CJ, Prentice A, Cole TJ. 2000. Risk factors for poor iron status in British toddlers: further analysis of data from the National Diet and Nutrition Survey of children aged 1^1/$_2$ to 4^1/$_2$ years. *Public Health Nutrition;* 3: 433-440.

29   Williams S, Sahota P. 1990. An enquiry into the attitudes of Muslim Asian mothers regarding infant feeding practices and dental health. *Journal of Human Nutrition and Dietetics;* 3: 393-402.

30   Sanders TAB. 1995. Vegetarian diets and children. *Pediatric Clinics of North America;* 42: 955-965.

31   Watt RG, Dykes J, Sheiham A. 2000. Drink consumption in British preschool children: relation to vitamin C, iron and calcium intakes. *Journal of Human Nutrition and Dietetics;* 13: 13-19.

32   Wall CR, Grant CC, Taua N, Wilson C, Thompson JM. 2005. Milk versus medicine for the treatment of iron deficiency anaemia in hospitalised infants. *Archives of Disease in Childhood;* 90: 1033-1038.

33   Scientific Advisory Committee on Nutrition. 2003. *Salt and Health.* London: TSO.

34   Gregory J, Lowe S, Bates CJ, Prentice A, Jackson LV, Smithers G, Wenlock R, Farron M. 2000. *National Diet and Nutrition Survey: Young People Aged 4-18 Years. Volume 1: Report of the Diet and Nutrition Survey.* London: TSO.

Chapter 4
Infant nutrition

This chapter summarises current advice on infant feeding and weaning. Infants are defined as those under the age of 12 months.

My baby sister drinking
Ella, aged 4

Nutrition in the early years of life is a major determinant of growth and development and it may also influence adult health. Weaning – the introduction of solid foods to babies as they become less dependent on milk – coincides with a period of rapid growth and development, so a good diet during this period is crucial. For sources of information about infant feeding, see Appendix 5.

Milk for babies

Infants up to 6 months of age receive all their nutritional requirements from breast milk or infant formula.

Breast milk

Breast milk is universally recognised as providing the best nutrition for babies and should be considered the method of choice for infant feeding. The balance of nutrients is uniquely ideal for a young baby and cannot be matched by a manufactured product. Breast milk is easily digested and hygienic and contains important antibodies that help babies to fight infections. In its *Infant Feeding Recommendation,*[1] the Department of Health recommends that babies are exclusively breastfed for the first 6 months (26 weeks) of life.

Evidence shows that infants who are breastfed experience fewer gastrointestinal and respiratory infections and are less likely to develop juvenile onset diabetes or to develop allergies, and there is some evidence that breastfed babies are less likely to be obese in later childhood.[1] In addition, breastfeeding mothers have a lower risk of developing pre-menopausal breast cancer, are more likely to return to their pre-pregnancy weight, and will have a delayed resumption of their menstrual cycle.

Breast milk can provide the main drink throughout the first year of life, and beyond, if mothers choose to continue breastfeeding. Breastfeeding mothers themselves should be well nourished and seek advice from health professionals to ensure that they are eating and drinking appropriately.

Mothers who return to work but who wish to continue providing breast milk for their babies should be encouraged to do so. Advice on expressing and storing breast milk can be obtained from a health visitor or breastfeeding counsellor. Breastfeeding support groups are available throughout the country through organisations such as the National Childbirth Trust, the Association of Breastfeeding Mothers and La Leche League. Contact details for these organisations are given in Appendix 5. For information about the responsibilities of employers, via health and safety legislation, to support breastfeeding mothers in the workplace, see the Equal Opportunities Commission website www.eoc-law.org.uk.

Advice for carers

- Carers should support breastfeeding mothers and encourage them to continue providing breast milk. Mothers who are breastfeeding and who may wish to feed their baby in the childcare setting should have warm, private facilities made available to them.

- Expressed breast milk provided for babies in child care should be clearly labelled with the child's name and the date, stored in a refrigerator and only be used for that child. Any expressed milk left over at the end of the day should be returned to the parent or guardian.

See also *Giving bottle feeds* on the right.

Carers should support breastfeeding mothers and encourage them to continue providing breast milk.

Infant formula

There are a number of artificial milks available for babies, called infant formula. If a baby is not being breastfed, only an appropriately modified formula baby milk can meet his or her nutritional needs. The advice given on the packet or tin must be followed. If there is any doubt about the suitability of the milk it is best to ask a health visitor for advice.

Infant formulas are usually manufactured from cow's milk but some are formulated from soya milk. Soy-based infant formula should only be used on the advice of a health professional or GP. Infant formula based on cow's milk comes in two types: whey dominant or casein dominant (depending on whether whey or casein is the dominant protein). Whey dominant infant formula has a protein content adjusted to remove much more of the casein from the cow's milk, which makes it a closer match to breast milk. Whey dominant formulas are usually suggested for very young babies. Casein dominant formulas are marketed as 'more satisfying' and many parents change to these milks as their babies get older, although there is no evidence to suggest that these milks are more suitable and there is anecdotal evidence that babies on this type of formula are more likely to be constipated.

Despite powerful marketing messages there is no manufactured breast milk

Giving bottle feeds

- Babies who are bottle-fed should be held and have warm physical contact with an attentive adult while being fed.

- Babies should never be left propped up with bottles as this is both dangerous and inappropriate to babies' emotional needs.

- Bottles, teats and cups used for infants under 6 months of age should be thoroughly cleaned and sterilised. The teats of bottles for older infants should be thoroughly cleaned.

- Recent guidance advises that bottle feeds should not be made up in advance and re-heated, but should be made up when required, using water at 70°C or above and cooled as appropriate.[2] If at any time bottles of liquid are heated, a microwave should not be used as the contents can become very hot even though the container still feels only warm.[3]

substitute which can mirror the composition of breast milk. Breast milk is the best food for babies, it is free, requires no preparation, is microbiologically safe and is always at the right temperature. If babies are not breastfed, infant formula is recommended as the main drink during the first year of life. Ordinary cow's milk is not suitable as a main drink before 12 months of age.

Advice for carers

- For those babies given infant formula it is essential that feeds are prepared correctly and safely. Because powdered infant formula is not sterile, wherever possible feeds should be made up freshly for each feed using boiled water that is hotter than 70°C. (This means water that has been boiled and left to cool for about 30 minutes.) Alternatively, ready-to-feed liquid formula can be used in childcare settings. Where parents wish to bring feeds made up from powdered formula to the childcare setting, storage times should be kept to a minimum. Feeds should be made as close as possible to feed time, cooled and stored at less than 5°C. If feeds are made up in advance, the made-up feeds should be stored for the minimum amount of time possible and not stored for longer than 24 hours.

- If the carer is making up infant formula, it is preferable if it can be made in a separate milk preparation area and the carer should ensure that hands are washed thoroughly and surfaces are clean. The manufacturer's instructions for making up the infant formula should be followed carefully. This includes using the correct amount of powder and water, using only freshly boiled water (either tap water or bottled water that is suitable for infants), and sterilising all equipment before use.

- Always discard the milk left in a bottle after a baby has finished feeding.

See also *Giving bottle feeds* on page 39.

Timing of feeds

Because children in the first year of life are following individual feeding and sleeping patterns, it is recommended that these are not disrupted but wherever possible integrated into the carer's timetable for the day.

Weaning (starting on solid foods)

Up to the age of about 6 months, breast milk or infant formula milk will provide all the nutrients and fluid that babies need. There is no need to give solids or non-milk drinks before about 6 months of age.[1] Breastfed babies do not need any additional fluids – including water – even if the weather is hot as they will demand more frequent feeds if they are thirsty and breast milk composition adapts to changing external temperatures. Formula-fed babies may need cooled boiled water to quench thirst if the weather is exceptionally hot, but this is not really necessary. Babies who appear hungrier at 4-6 months and change their sleeping routines may require more frequent breast or formula milk feeds to satisfy them.

There remains, however, some confusion about when babies should be weaned. The Department of Health recommends that babies should not be given any solid foods until they are 6 months of age.[1] However, some manufacturers' literature and some health professionals suggest weaning from 4 months of age. Research suggests that currently about half of parents wean before 4 months of age, so it may take some time for the recommended pattern of weaning at about 6 months to become established in the UK.[4] Many health professionals prefer to advise parents to wean when their children show develop-mental cues such as being able to sit up with some support, having some trunk control, showing an active interest in food and having the ability to pick food up and put it to their mouth, rather than by age alone. Weaning before 4 months of age is never recommended, but since the

majority of families in the UK are currently starting to give their babies solids before 6 months of age, specific recommendations on the foods to avoid for infants under 6 months of age are given on the next page.

From about 6 months of age, the majority of infants are able to take food from a spoon, chew and use the tongue. They will also at this stage be curious about other tastes and textures and develop their hand-to-eye coordination. By about 6 months of age an infant can also have finger foods. There is no evidence that waiting until 6 months to wean will affect a baby's ability to chew. When the baby seems ready to experiment, small spoonfuls of baby rice, puréed vegetables such as carrots or peas or mashed potato can be offered. Some babies will take time to learn to take food from a spoon, so it is important to go at the baby's pace and smile encouragement as he or she learns. Babies weaned at about 6 months usually accept a greater variety of foods and changes in food textures more quickly than those weaned earlier.

All babies should have started on solid foods by around 6 months of age since at this stage babies need more iron and other nutrients than can be provided by milk alone. Parents of babies who were born prematurely need individual advice about when to start solid foods. Resources on feeding and weaning premature babies can be found in Appendix 5.

Certain foods can cause an allergic reaction in some babies. It is therefore recommended that babies should not be given certain foods before 6 months of age. See the box on the next page.

Rice or oat cereals are acceptable and should be given from a

Foods to avoid before 6 months of age

It is recommended that first foods given to infants younger than 6 months are 'gluten-free' foods. Gluten is found in foods such as bread, pasta or chapatis made from wheat.

Nuts and seeds – including peanuts, peanut butter and other nut spreads – should be avoided by all infants under 6 months. If babies come from a family where parents, brothers or sisters have allergic conditions such as asthma, eczema or hayfever (known as atopic families), government advice[5] is that peanuts and peanut products should be avoided for the first three years of life. Mothers in atopic families should also avoid peanuts and peanut products during pregnancy and when breastfeeding.

Eggs, raw or cooked shellfish, shark, swordfish and marlin, citrus fruit and juices should also be avoided until 6 months of age.

Foods containing plant sterols (eg. some margarines and yoghurts) should not be given to under-5s. The ingredients label will indicate if the food contains plant sterols.

Honey should not be given to children under the age of 12 months.

spoon. Foods should not be added to bottles of milk as this does not allow the infant to learn how food feels in the mouth or how to chew, and it may cause choking. Manufactured weaning foods (bought in packets, jars or tins) can be chosen according to the baby's age. It is important to offer a good variety of tastes so that infants get used to different flavours.

One particularly important nutrient for babies is iron, as by 6 months the body stores of iron that an infant is born with have been used up, and the baby needs to obtain iron from the diet. (The importance of iron in the diet is discussed in detail on page 32.) Good sources of iron which can be given as purées or mash are: meat; fish such as tuna or sardines; pulses such as peas, beans and lentils; and green vegetables. The iron from meat and some fish is easily absorbed into the body and a daily helping of these foods is a valuable way of providing iron in the weaning diet.

Texture is also important. First foods should be of purée consistency but as soon as babies are used to taking food from a spoon, chewing and swallowing, they can be given soft lumps or food which is mashed rather than puréed. As eating and chewing skills increase, minced or finely chopped foods and finger foods should be given and different textures of food should be introduced. By about 12 months, children should be getting a good mixed diet with three meals and, depending on their sleeping patterns and appetite, one or two healthy snacks each day.

It is recommended that breastfed babies from 6 months of age (or from 1 month of age if mothers did not eat well during pregnancy), and formula-fed babies once their milk intake drops to 500ml a day, should be given vitamin drops containing vitamins A, C and D. Parents or guardians can get further information from their health visitor or GP.

Weaning tips

Up-to-date information on what foods should be avoided during weaning can be found on www.eatwell.gov.uk.

- Soft cooked meat, fish and pulses (such as peas, beans and lentils) are suitable and important foods to include in the diet from 6 months.

- Offer a variety of flavours and soft textures. Between 6 months and 1 year, give food which allows the infant to learn to chew and accept a wide variety of food textures.

- Eggs given to babies or toddlers should be cooked until both the yolk and the white are solid.

- If using commercial weaning foods, follow the manufacturer's instructions carefully.

- Whole cow's milk can be used as an ingredient in weaning foods, for example to moisten mashed potato, but cow's milk should not be the main drink for infants under 1 year.

- As weaning progresses, introduce soft lumps, and finger foods.

- Do not add salt to foods for infants.

- Do not add sugar to foods for infants. Instead use naturally sweet fruits such as apples or bananas

- Do not add artificial sweeteners to food for infants.

Vitamin D and exposure to sunlight

Exposure to summer sunlight in outdoor play helps children to maintain their vitamin D status. However, childcare settings should have a 'sun policy', with guidelines on how long children can remain outdoors in strong sunshine and on the use of protective clothing such as sunhats, and sunscreen. All under-5s should be appropriately supervised at all times while outdoors.

Drinks for infants

From 6 months of age infants should be introduced to drinking from a cup or beaker. From the age of 1 year, they should be discouraged from drinking from a bottle.

Use an open cup or beaker rather than one which requires the infant to suck the drink (sometimes called a 'dinky feeder' or a 'non-spill' cup). This is because sucking drinks across the teeth can contribute to tooth damage (see page 51).

Tap water is suitable from 6 months of age but should be boiled and cooled for younger infants.

Adult-type soft drinks, low-sugar drinks or 'diet' drinks, tea and coffee should not be given to infants.

Frequent use of fruit drinks, including baby juices and other baby drinks, should be discouraged as they encourage a sweet tooth and can contribute to dental disease.

If drinks other than milk or water are given (for example, diluted baby juices or baby drinks), these should be diluted with at least 10 parts of water and confined to mealtimes. Because of the risk to dental health, they should never be given in a feeding bottle.

Hygiene and safety tips

- If dummies or comforters are used, they should be thoroughly cleaned and sterilised for infants under 6 months, and thoroughly cleaned for older infants. This also applies to dummies or comforters which are dropped.

- Artificial milk feeds should be made up using boiled water that is hotter than 70°C. (This means water that has been boiled and left to cool for about 30 minutes.)

- Artificial milk feeds should be made up fresh for each feed and left-over milk should be thrown away.

- The kettle should be filled with fresh tap water before boiling water for making up infant formula. If you are using bottled water, only use bottled water suitable for infants. These will say on the label that they are suitable for infant feeding.

- If you are serving food from a can or jar and the child is unlikely to eat all the contents, spoon a portion into a separate dish or container before serving it to the child. Store any unused portions according to the manufacturer's instructions. If there are no instructions, the safest option is to throw the unused portion away. If food is served straight from the jar and the child does not finish it, the remainder should be thrown away.

- Any uneaten food which parents have brought in should be returned to them at the end of the day.

- Do not use unpasteurised milk, or milk-based products such as cheese and yoghurt that are made from unpasteurised milk or mould-ripened (blue-veined) cheeses.

- Fruits and vegetables to be eaten raw should be well washed before eating. Carrots should be topped and peeled. Fruit and vegetables should be peeled for younger infants, to prevent choking.

- Whole pieces of nut should not be given to infants or children under 5 in case of choking.

- Never leave children or infants alone while they are eating in case they choke.

References

1 Department of Health. 2003. *Infant Feeding Recommendation*. Accessed from www.dh.gov.uk

2 www.food.gov.uk

3 Puczynski M, Rademaker D, Gatson R. 1983. Burn injury related to improper use of microwave ovens. *Paediatrics;* 72: 5.

4 Hamlyn B, Brooker J, Oleinikova K, Wands S. 2002. *Infant Feeding 2000*. London: TSO.

5 Department of Health. 1998. *Report on Peanut Allergy. Committee on Toxicity of Chemicals in Food, Consumer Products and the Environment (COT)*. London: TSO.

Chapter 5
Encouraging children to eat well

This chapter gives some practical guidelines on how to encourage under-5s in child care to eat well. It looks at the types of foods and drinks to offer, and gives information on vegetarian diets, special diets, food safety and hygiene issues, timing of meals and snacks and how carers can involve parents and guardians to ensure that children eat well.

I eat an apple for my snack
Siân, aged 5

Eating a variety of foods

The role of different nutrients in ensuring good health has been described in chapter 3. One of the basic principles to ensure healthy eating is to eat a variety of foods. It is easier to get all the vitamins and minerals needed for good health if a good variety of foods is eaten. It is difficult to achieve adequate intakes of vitamins and minerals when diets are monotonous and based on few foods.[1] A varied diet is also associated with better health.[2]

Children do not have an inborn ability to select a balanced and nutritious diet[3] but increasing the variety of available foods should increase the number of different foods chosen. Parents and carers often allow a child's initial rejection of a new food to determine whether that food is offered again, yet research has shown that continued exposure to a food will increase the likelihood that the child will eat it.[4] It has been shown, however, that a new food will not be chosen unless the child has tasted it, which suggests that it is important to encourage children to taste all the foods offered at a meal.[5] Parents or guardians, particularly those on low incomes, may be unwilling to experiment with new foods which may be rejected and then thrown away. Carers can often offer a wider choice and may therefore play an important part in encouraging a varied diet.

As children get older they are generally willing to eat a wider variety of foods, and snacks become an increasingly important source of energy and nutrients. The innate preference for foods which are sweet is particularly observed in childhood. Children who are given early and consistent exposure to sweet tastes may reject other tastes.

It is important that foods offered to children as snacks are also varied. Although biscuits and crisps are eaten regularly by about 80% of children between 1½ and 4½ years,[6] these are not the only or the most nutritious snacks available. Snack foods can be based on a variety of cereals and cereal products as well as on fruits and vegetables. Some ideas for a variety of different snack foods are given on the right, and on page 55.

Eating a varied diet

Children should be encouraged to eat a varied diet. They should eat foods from each of the four main food groups every day. The four main food groups are:

- bread, other cereals and potatoes
- fruit and vegetables
- milk and dairy foods, and
- meat, fish and alternatives such as pulses (peas, beans and lentils), eggs, vegetable proteins and soya.

A varied diet is associated with better health as it is more likely to contain all the vitamins and minerals the body needs.

There are some vitamins and minerals which have been shown to be consumed by children in amounts below the Reference Nutrient Intakes. These include vitamins A and C and the minerals iron and zinc. Increasing the amounts of different meats, fish, cereals and fruit and vegetables in the diet is likely to improve the intake of all these nutrients. Diets which are not varied are often particularly low in fruit and vegetable foods. Children from poorer families are more likely to have a low intake of fruit and vegetables.[7]

Fruit and vegetables

Fruit and vegetables are now thought to be particularly important for good health. In adults the antioxidant nutrients they contain protect against chronic diseases such as coronary heart disease and cancer. Under-5s should be encouraged to have tastes of at least five different fruits and vegetables every day to accustom them to eating these foods when they get older.[8] Very young children may only be able to manage small amounts but those over 2 years of age should be offered child-sized portions with all meals and with some snacks.

Suggested fruits and vegetables for mealtimes

½ to 1 heaped tablespoon of cooked vegetables such as peas, sweetcorn, carrots, cabbage, courgettes or swede

½ to 1 heaped tablespoon of beans such as butter beans, chick peas or lentils

1-2 broccoli or cauliflower florets

4-5 green beans

Small handful of salad leaves

¼ -½ sweet potato

1 small parsnip

Small slice of squash or marrow

½ tablespoon of dried fruit

1-2 tablespoons of stewed fruit

1-2 tablespoons of canned fruit in juice

100-150ml 100% diluted fruit juice

Suggested fruits and vegetables for snacks

½ medium carrot cut into sticks

2-3cm piece of cucumber in sticks

1 small celery stick cut into pieces

4 cherry tomatoes or 4 small tomato quarters

1 ring of red, yellow or green pepper

½ to 1 small banana

½ apple or pear

1 plum

½ to 1 kiwi

¼ -½ large orange or 1 small orange, clementine or satsuma

1 small slice of melon or pineapple

1 tablespoon of berries such as blackberries, raspberries or fresh currants

4-6 strawberries

8-10 grapes

It is worth experimenting with different vegetables and vegetable dishes to find those that are acceptable. Some children may reject cabbage but enjoy 'bubble and squeak' (cabbage and potato mixed together). Others may find stir-fry vegetables more interesting than boiled ones. Carrots, red peppers and sweetcorn are appealing in colour, taste and texture. Peas are a popular and familiar vegetable for most children. Some children like raw vegetables more than cooked ones. There is some evidence that children aged 2-6 years who are exposed to repeated tasting of vegetables over 14 days will increasingly accept and enjoy them.[9]

Food for all

Food is an important part of everyone's lives. Eating together, having special foods and avoiding particular foods are all intimately related to aspects of people's family life, cultural, religious and intellectual beliefs. It is important to recognise that the food available for any group of people should be appropriate and familiar. It is essential to involve parents or guardians in the choice of foods provided in child care: good communication between parents and those providing child care is vital.

When planning meals for any group of people, the particular needs of that group must be considered. Cultural and religious differences are commonly expressed in food preferences and food avoidances. Providing the right ingredients is not the only factor to consider: food should look and taste familiar as well.

All food activities should allow for cultural differences: activities involving food give children the opportunity to learn about new and different foods. Holidays, festivals and religious celebrations of various cultures provide a valuable opportunity to celebrate differences in food experiences.

Some of the differences in food choice commonly observed by those from different religious and cultural groups are summarised in Appendix 4. It is important to emphasise that there may be individual differences in food choices between families, and those providing child care should not make assumptions about anyone's food preferences. It is important to find out about each child from his or her parent or guardian.

All children, and their parents or guardians, should be respected as individuals, and their food preferences and religious requirements should be accommodated.

All that children bring with them to their place of child care – their race, gender, family background, language, culture and religion – should be valued in order for children to feel accepted and accepting of themselves. It is therefore important to value the contributions which different cultures and nationalities make to the variety of foods eaten in the UK today.

Physical activity

Physical activity is a term used to describe body movement. It includes:

- everyday body movements such as walking, playing, or climbing stairs, and

- movement which is often described as 'exercise'. For children this might be, for example, running, playing football, or playing in a playground.

The more the body moves, the more energy (or calories) is used up. The relationship between energy (calorie) intake and physical activity is explained on page 20.

Activity can be encouraged both indoors and outdoors. Outdoor play gives children the opportunity to 'let off steam' and provides many more opportunities for them to be physically active. Most children are attracted to outdoor play if they are offered a range of suitable activities.

The Department of Health recommends that all children from 2 years of age should achieve a minimum of 60 minutes of moderate intensity activity every day. ('Moderate intensity' means enough to make them feel warm and slightly out of breath.) At least twice a week this should include activities that improve bone health, muscle strength and flexibility.[10] It is essential that there is outdoor space where children can play, or access to an outside area such as a garden, park or other safe open space. Carers need to timetable periods of activity into the children's daily routine and encourage children to be active throughout the year. Children in child care should also have access to toys for active play – for example balls, hoops and skipping ropes.

Carers should ensure that outdoor play equipment is safe. All children should be closely supervised during sand and water play and should not be left alone while playing outdoors. Carers should be aware that some children's dress may restrict them in outdoor play and it may be necessary to sensitively adjust their clothing for outdoor activities. Children playing outside should be appropriately dressed for cold or rainy weather with coats and jackets buttoned up and scarves, mittens, boots and hats used as necessary. Information about improving outdoor play for pre-school children can be obtained from the organisation Learning Through Landscapes (see page 84).

Exposure to summer sunlight in outdoor play helps children to maintain their vitamin D status. However, childcare settings should have a 'sun policy', with guidelines on how long children can remain outdoors in strong sunshine, and on the use of protective clothing such as sunhats, and sunscreen.

Why it is important for children to be physically active

- The more energy children use up, the more food they will need to eat. A child who is inactive may have a very small appetite and may not be able to get all the nutrients he or she needs in a small amount of food.

- Exposure to summer sunlight in outdoor play helps children to maintain their vitamin D status (see page 28).

- Physical activity builds up muscle strength and overall fitness, and develops physical skills such as balance, coordination and climbing skills.

- A considerable amount of learning can take place while children are playing outdoors. For example, they learn about the environment around them, and interacting with other children can contribute to their confidence.

Worries about fatness in children

Parents or guardians who are concerned about their child being or becoming fat should encourage and enable the child to increase the amount of exercise he or she does each day. This can include activities done as part of the daily routine such as walking and climbing stairs, as well as physically active play such as running, ball games or playing in a playground. They may also want to restrict the amount of inactivity among under-5s since the amount of television viewed is typically a strong predictor of body weight.[11]

Children are unlikely to become fat if they eat, while in child care, the amount and types of food recommended in this report and if they follow the general advice it gives about healthy eating and physical activity. However, if a child eats a significant amount of other foods as 'extras' – particularly if these are high in calories but contain few other nutrients (for example sweets, biscuits, cakes, savoury snacks or soft drinks) – the child may take in more calories than they use up in their daily activities.

Restricting food intake among children (ie. giving them less to eat than they would choose, or using 'low-calorie' foods that are designed for adults) may prevent children from getting all the nutrients they need for normal growth and development. If parents or guardians have concerns about their child's weight, they should ask their GP or health visitor for advice. The GP might refer the family to a dietitian.

Drinks for the under-5s

Milk

Milk is the main source of calcium for the under-5s and it also contributes substantially to the protein, riboflavin, vitamin A, iodine and zinc intakes of children in this age group. Children aged between 12 months and 2 years should be given whole milk. Semi-skimmed milk can be introduced gradually after the age of 2 years, provided that the child is a good eater and has a varied diet.

Skimmed milk is not suitable as a main drink for children under 5 years of age, as it does not contain enough calories or vitamins.

Some children may reject milk unless some flavouring is added. Flavoured milk is usually sweetened in some way and, while this may be a useful way of encouraging milk drinking in some children, it is better that flavoured sweetened drinks are drunk with meals, rather than between meals, because of the risk to teeth.

Some children cannot drink cow's milk. For those over 1 year this may be substituted with goat's milk or soya drinks, but these are not suitable for infants. In addition it is important to note that goat's milk is not a suitable alternative for children who are allergic to cow's milk as the proteins in the milk are similar and it could cause a reaction. Some of the alternative milks available are described on the right. There is no health advantage in giving milks other than cow's milk to children who can tolerate cow's milk.

The Department of Health's Welfare Food Scheme enables children under 5 to receive, free of charge, one-third of a pint (189ml) of milk for each day they attend approved day care facilities for 2 hours or more. Day care providers who have been approved to supply milk under the scheme can be reimbursed the cost of the milk they supply. This scheme will not be changed by the new Healthy Start scheme. Providers can apply direct to the Welfare Food Reimbursement Unit[12] (WFRU) to take part in the scheme. Some local authorities administer the scheme centrally on behalf of some pre-schools. This provision is in addition to the milk tokens available through the Welfare Food Scheme, and the vouchers for milk, fruit and vegetables and infant formula that will be available through its replacement scheme Healthy Start. (See www.healthystart.nhs.uk for details.)

Which milks to give under-5s as a main drink

Infants = children under 12 months

Breast milk	The best milk for infants.
Infant formula	Cow's milk specially modified for infants is labelled as such. Follow the instructions given on the packet or tin when choosing and preparing infant formula.
Follow-on infant formula	Modified cow's milk only suitable for infants from 6 months of age.
Soya infant formula	May be given from birth but only if advised by a doctor. These formulas contain sugar in the form of glucose which is more harmful to teeth than the lactose in infant formula based on cow's milk. Care should be taken that infants are not left with bottles for long periods and children should be given soya infant formula in cups, preferably with meals.
Whole cow's milk*	Not suitable for infants. Suitable for most children from 12 months of age.
Semi-skimmed cow's milk*	Not suitable for infants or children under 2 years, but can be introduced gradually after the age of 2 years, provided that the child is a good eater and has a varied diet.
Skimmed cow's milk*, including dried skimmed milks	Not suitable for infants or children under 5 years.
Evaporated milk	Not suitable for infants. Skimmed milk varieties are not suitable for children.
Condensed milk	Not suitable for infants or children.
Soya drinks (other than soya infant formula)	Not suitable for infants. If children are given soya drinks, make sure the drink is calcium-fortified. Drinks should be given in cups because of the sugars content.
Goat's milk*	Not suitable for infants unless recommended by a paediatrician.
Cow's milk substitutes such as oat milk, rice milk or almond milk	Not suitable for children under 5 as these drinks are low in calcium and protein and may have added sugar.

* Milks given to under-5s should be pasteurised.

Soft drinks

There is a wide range of soft drinks available, most of which are sweetened with sugars, sweeteners (for example saccharin or aspartame), and commonly a mixture of both. They include:

- squashes and other drinks which need to be diluted

- carbonated soft drinks such as cola or lemonade, and

- fruit drinks which are drinks that contain a proportion of fruit juice as well as water and some form of sugar and/or sweetener.

Children can be conditioned at an early age to the sweet taste of drinks. High intakes of soft drinks have been reported to lead to frequent looser stools, poor appetites and failure to thrive.[13] Data from the National Diet and Nutrition Survey showed that among under-5s soft drinks are consumed more frequently than milk, 56% of under-5s consume soft drinks more than once a day, and children obtain a third of their sugar intake from drinks alone.[14]

Tap water is suitable for children and should always be the drink of choice for quenching thirst.

Soft drinks containing sweeteners are generally not recommended for children. If soft drinks (such as squashes) containing saccharin are given to the under-5s they should be diluted much more than they would be for an adult – for example, a dilution of 1 part squash to at least 10 parts water.

Soft drinks containing sugar can be harmful to the teeth, especially if they are drunk frequently or stay in contact with the teeth for too long. If sugary drinks are given, they should be kept to mealtimes. Soft drinks such as fruit drinks and fruit squashes should not be given at bedtime or during the night as this practice increases the risk of dental decay.

Soft drinks labelled 'low-sugar' or 'no added sugar' may still harm children's teeth as they often do contain some sugar and they may also be acidic. This is also true for baby herbal drinks. Any of the following on the ingredients label of a soft drink indicates that the drink has sugar added: glucose, glucose syrup, fructose, concentrated fruit juice, sucrose, dextrose, honey, invert sugar, maltose, hydrolysed starch.

Sweetened fizzy drinks such as cola or lemonade are both sugary and acidic. The 'diet' versions of these drinks can also be harmful to teeth even if they do not contain sugar, as the acidity erodes the dental enamel.

Many ready-to-drink cartons of squashes, fruit drinks or fruit juices have a high sugar content and cannot be diluted if they are drunk straight from the carton, and children who are regularly given full strength drinks may become used to the intensity of the sweetness. Children who bring their own drinks to child care should be encouraged to bring a plastic flask or a lidded plastic cup containing an appropriately diluted drink.

Pure unsweetened (100%) fruit juices

Pure fruit juices are a good source of vitamin C as well as some other nutrients. They are most beneficial when given with meals, as this may help the body absorb iron. However, fruit juices have also been shown to be acidic enough to erode dental enamel in young children so it is best to avoid giving them between meals and, when giving them to under-5s, it is best to dilute them with plenty of water.

Some fruit juice drinks are available which contain some fruit juice, with added sugar and water. These are not a good choice for under-5s. Fruit juice drinks which have been fortified with a range of extra vitamins and minerals are not suitable for children. Always check the label to see if the drink is marked 'unsuitable for children'.

Water

Tap water is suitable for children and should always be the drink of choice for quenching thirst. Some bottled waters may have a high content of salts, so cooled tap water is the best option. It has been reported that parents and carers do not like giving water to children as they think children will reject it, that it is 'cruel', and that offering water is a sign of poverty.[15] It is important therefore that carers are positive about water drinking, make sure that palatable water is always available, act as role models for water drinking, and encourage children to serve water to each other. Children in child care may enjoy having their own water bottles to drink out of during the day. These should be clearly marked with their name and refilled daily with fresh, cooled tap water.

Other drinks

Tea and coffee are not recommended as a drink for infants or children as the tannic acid they contain reduces the absorption of iron.[16] However, it is recognised that some children in child care are given milky tea as a way of encouraging them to drink milk. If tea is used in this way it should be very weak.

Which drinks to give

Drinks should be given in an open cup or beaker. Do not use feeder cups (sometimes called 'dinky feeders' or 'non-spill cups') which children must suck on to get their drinks as sucking drinks across the teeth can contribute to tooth damage and mimic the action of drinking from bottles. 'Doidy' cups (which have a naturally tilting front edge to make drinking easy for very young children) are recommended by many health professionals and can be obtained from the National Childbirth Trust. (For details see *Equipment* on page 86.)

• Encourage children to drink water if they are thirsty. Water quenches thirst, does not spoil the appetite, and does not damage teeth. Tap water is preferable as some bottled waters have a high content of salts and may not be suitable.

• Promote milk as a drink in a cup. Whole cow's milk is suitable as a main drink for most children from 12 months of age. Semi-skimmed milk can be introduced after the age of 2 years, provided that the child is a good eater. Skimmed milk is not suitable as the main drink for a child under 5 years of age. Drinking too much milk is associated with poor iron status. Up to about three-quarters of a pint (around 450ml) of milk each day is likely to be fine.

• Diluted fruit juice is a useful source of vitamin C. Children should be encouraged to have a glass of diluted fruit juice with their main meal or with breakfast as this may also help the body to absorb iron (see page 32).

• Discourage children from having fizzy drinks and squashes (including fruit squashes and fruit drinks), both diet and non-diet, as these can erode the tooth enamel and contribute to tooth decay. Also, they provide little in the way of nutrients, and children who drink them frequently may have less appetite to eat well at mealtimes.

• Tea and coffee are not suitable drinks for under-5s as they contain tannic acid which interferes with iron absorption.

Dental health among the under-5s

The role of non-milk extrinsic sugars (NME sugars) in dental health is described on page 23. It is accepted that dental decay is directly related to the frequency and amount of NME sugar consumption.[17] There is a popular myth that it does not matter if children have tooth decay in their first teeth. This is not the case. Tooth decay in a child's first teeth:

• can affect the development of the permanent teeth

• can cause infections and swelling which can be painful and lead to sleepless nights, and

• may involve the need to extract teeth under anaesthetic.

The incidence of dental disease in young children in the UK decreased dramatically in the 1970s due to the introduction and use of fluoride toothpastes but since then reductions have slowed down. In 2003, 40% of 5 year olds had some experience of dental decay and 53% had signs of tooth surface loss caused by erosion.[18] High intakes of soft drinks are likely to be directly causative in both decay and tooth surface loss, and studies show that children put to bed with a sugary drink, those who brush their own teeth without supervision, and those who use bottles for drinks are at greatest risk.[19]

To reduce the risk of decay, it is important to reduce the amount of time that teeth are exposed to foods high in non-milk extrinsic sugars. This includes foods such as sweets, biscuits, cakes and sugary cereals as well as soft drinks. Fresh fruit is a good choice as a snack, but fruit juice and dried fruit do contain significant amounts of non-milk

How carers can help reduce tooth decay in children

- Reduce the total amount and especially the frequency of sugary foods and drinks that children have.

- If children are having sugary foods and drinks, these should be given with meals rather than between meals. This is because children's first teeth are prone to decay if they are frequently in contact with sugars. Using a straw with drinks may reduce the contact of the drink with the teeth.

- To help the healthy development of teeth, children should not be given sweet drinks (such as fruit juice, fruit juice drinks, squashes and other soft drinks) in a feeding bottle, dinky feeder or non-spill cup. An open cup or beaker should be used if these drinks are given with meals.

- If a child uses a dummy or comforter, never dip it into sugar or sugary drinks as this will contribute to tooth decay.

- Some soft drinks which claim to have 'no added sugar' still contain sugars which are harmful to the teeth. Diet drinks, both fizzy and still, can also be harmful to the teeth. This is because they may be acidic and erode the dental enamel, especially if sipped frequently. The use of these drinks should be avoided or limited.

- Milk and water are the only safe drinks for children's teeth. Flavoured milks with added sugar should only be served with meals.

- It is generally not advised that children brush their teeth while in child care but they should be encouraged to do this at home.

Additional advice for parents of under-5s

- Brush children's teeth daily with a pea-sized blob of fluoride toothpaste. Children whose teeth are brushed by their parents or carers have less plaque.[21] Toothbrushing should be supervised by an adult for children up to 7 years of age. Children should spit out the toothpaste, but not rinse their mouths after brushing.

- Fluoride supplements can be given to children who are at high risk of dental decay. Parents should ask their child's dentist if this is necessary.

- Children should start visiting the dentist regularly by 3 years of age. (Dental check-ups and treatment are free up to the age of 18, or up to 19 if they are in full-time education.)

- Choose sugar-free medicines where possible. If a GP is prescribing medicines, the parent should ask the GP or pharmacist if a sugar-free version is available.

- Soft drinks such as fruit drinks and fruit squashes should never be given at bedtime or during the night as these are particularly associated with dental decay.

extrinsic sugars so they should be consumed with meals rather than between meals.[20]

Carers should ask parents and guardians the name and contact details of the child's dentist when they register with them for child care. This will help to prompt them to register their child with a dentist if they have not already done so. NHS Direct will put parents in touch with an NHS dentist in their area. (For details, see page 85.)

Commercial foods for babies and children

There are a wide variety of baby and toddler foods available from commercial manufacturers, many of which can be a useful choice when time or facilities for food preparation are limited. While there are strict guidelines ensuring that baby foods sold for infants (under 1 year of age) are not too high in salt and that they do not contain certain pesticide residues,[22] foods for under-1s are often still high in sugars.

There are no similar guidelines for foods for children over 1 year of age and many baby food 'snacks', such as biscuits, sold as suitable for children over 1 are very high in sugar. Intakes of these snack foods should be treated in the same way as for any equivalent adult foods. Carers should look at food labels carefully and choose baby foods and snacks that are lower in salt and sugar. Baby foods are also very expensive and do not offer good value for money compared with home-made foods. For ideas for snacks for under-5s, see page 55.

Vegetarian diets

Children can get the energy and nutrients they need from a vegetarian diet but a little extra care is needed. Nutrient-rich foods such as milk, cheese and eggs can provide protein, vitamin A, calcium and zinc but obtaining enough iron from a meat-free diet may be more difficult. If the child eats fish, iron can be found in oily fish such as sardines, pilchards and tuna. Iron is also found in pulses such as beans and lentils, in dried fruit and in breakfast cereals. The iron may be more easily absorbed if the child has foods or drinks that are high in vitamin C – for example fruits, vegetables or juices – at the same meal. Tea and coffee should not be given as these can interfere with the absorption of iron. A vegetarian diet which provides a variety of cereal foods, vegetables, pulses, fruits and dairy products is likely to supply sufficient nutrients.

The vitamin drops obtained at child health centres are suitable for vegetarians but may not be acceptable to strict vegans as the vitamin D is sourced from sheep's wool. (For more on vitamin drops, see page 28.)

When cooking food for vegetarians who exclude food items for religious or ethical reasons, it is important that the food given is not compromised in any way. For example, picking meat out of a dish is not acceptable – the vegetarian dish should be prepared first and the meat added later for other children. Care should be taken with ingredients such as gelatine, lard or suet, and labels should be checked for animal fats and animal rennet.

Information and advice on ingredients to avoid can be obtained from the Vegetarian Society (see page 85).

Vegan diets

Vegan diets are outside the scope of this report. Parents of vegan children must take their own responsibility for their children's diets and can get advice from the Vegan Society (see page 85).

Special diets

Some children have special dietary requirements. Special diets are the foods recommended by a registered dietitian or doctor for a specific medical condition. Children with coeliac disease for example cannot tolerate gluten, the protein in wheat flour as well as in a number of other cereals including barley and rye, and they require a gluten-free diet. If a child has a recognised special diet, the parent or guardian should be able to supply a list of acceptable foods, and in some cases can provide the foods themselves. A careful plan for choosing a safe and nutritious diet for the individual child needs to be drawn up in consultation with a registered dietitian.

Dairy-free diets

Dairy-free diets may be necessary for children who are lactose intolerant or have a cow's milk protein intolerance.

Lactose is the sugar naturally occurring in milk and all milk-based foods. Lactose intolerance is commonly found in some Asian and African populations. It is caused by a deficiency of lactase – the enzyme required to digest lactose – and it causes unpleasant digestive symptoms including diarrhoea.

Some children may be intolerant to cow's milk protein. One study on the Isle of Wight showed that cow's milk intolerance was found in 4.4% of children aged 1 year, 1.9% of children aged 2 years, and 0.4 % of children aged 4 years.[23]

Milk and other dairy foods provide a substantial amount of calcium, iodine and riboflavin in the diets of children. Infants and children up to 2 years who do not have milk or dairy products should continue on the infant formula recommended to them by a doctor or a registered dietitian. After the age of 2, if soya products are acceptable, children can be given a soya drink which has been fortified with calcium (found by checking the label). Other sources of non-dairy calcium are soya-based foods such as tofu, tempeh and soya mince or soya cheese, soya drink fortified with calcium, canned sardines or salmon (including the bones), pilchards, egg yolk, bread, breakfast cereals, pulses (such as beans, lentils and chick peas), dark green leafy vegetables, sesame seeds, sesame paste, ground almonds and dried fruit.

The parent or guardian should be able to provide a list of foods which are milk-product-free.

Food allergy

Food allergy can be defined as a reproducible adverse reaction to a food involving the immune system. In food allergy there is an abnormal sensitivity to a substance present in food (usually a protein) which is generally considered harmless for the majority of people. Reactions can be severe and in rare cases life-threatening, but most people grow out of food allergies in early childhood.

Chilcare settings should have an allergy plan in place. Information for pre-school settings on how to manage allergic children can be found on www.allergyinschools.org.uk.

Foods that can cause severe allergic reactions include: peanuts, nuts, shellfish, sesame seeds, cow's milk, eggs, fish, citrus fruits, soya beans, wheat and other cereals. Food allergies are more likely to occur in children with a family history of allergies such as asthma, eczema or hay fever.

While many parents believe that their children are sensitive to certain foods, the true incidence is likely to be very much lower than reported. Parents requesting special diets for their children because of food allergy should be encouraged to seek advice from a doctor or a registered dietitian if they have not already done so. It is unwise to restrict food choice among young children without appropriate help and advice.

However, it is important to note that a Department of Health Expert Panel recommends that, in children with a family history of atopic disease (asthma, eczema, hay fever or food allergy), peanuts and peanut products should be avoided until the child is 3 years old.[24] For children who are advised to avoid nuts in foods, careful checking of food labels will be required. New labelling regulations require that whenever certain allergenic ingredients (including tree nuts and peanuts) or products derived from them are used in pre-packed foods, the label must clearly indicate that they are present in the food.[25] For those children who are advised to avoid nuts in foods, these ingredients can be identified by looking carefully at the ingredients of pre-packed foods.

The following are some of the names given to nuts or nut products: nuts, chipped nuts, flaked nuts, peanuts, groundnuts, monkey nuts, earthnuts, arachis

Ensuring that the diet is of good quality should be a priority rather than buying expensive nutrient supplements.

hypogaea, arachis oil, groundnut oil, peanut oil, peanut butter, nut butters, nut paste, marzipan, praline, frangipane, goober peas, pinder, goober, nut flavours, nut extract, hydrolysed vegetable oils or proteins, nut oil derivatives or additives such as E471, E472 or lecithin. Foods purchased without labels (for example food bought unpackaged in shops or from open markets) should always be treated with caution.

Diet, behaviour and learning in children

There is significant current interest in whether the diet can influence children's behaviour and ability to learn and concentrate. Overall, research in this area suggests that a good, varied diet is the best way to ensure optimal mental and behavioural performance in children, and that only those children who have very poor nutritional status (for example, those with severe iron deficiency anaemia) may benefit from dietary manipulation.[26] There is insubstantial evidence that giving children fish oil supplements impacts on their performance. Ensuring that the diet is of good quality should be a priority rather than buying expensive nutrient supplements.

Children with special needs

Children with special needs and physical disabilities should whenever possible be encouraged to eat the same healthy diet in the same way as all other children. When planning food provision and menus, carers need to consider any children in their care who have special needs so that they can feel included at

meal and snack times. Some children may have particular dietary requirements or may need specific help with eating, both of which are outside the scope of this report. Advice can be obtained from a registered dietitian. Parents or guardians and carers may also find it useful to contact support groups associated with the child's particular disability or need.

Food safety and good hygiene

Food provided to under-5s should be stored, prepared and presented in a safe and hygienic environment. Extra care is needed for infants and young children as they may have a lower resistance to food poisoning.

Carers should always wash their hands with soap and water before preparing food or helping children to eat, and after changing nappies and toileting children. If carers use a handkerchief while preparing food, they should wash their hands before continuing.

All work surfaces and utensils used in the preparation of food should be clean.

Carers need to be aware of the requirements of the Food Safety Act. Some carers may need to complete a Food Hygiene Certificate course. Further information on this can be obtained from the local authority's environmental health department, or from its registration and inspection unit.

Carers also need to be aware of food hygiene and food safety to prevent food contamination and food poisoning. They need to know about storage of food and leftover food, and thorough cooking or heating of foods. Several useful publications are

53

available from the Food Standards Agency (see Appendix 5). Carers should obtain these and follow the advice in them. Some of the main points for carers are given in the box below.

It is also important that children are taught basic hygiene themselves – for example not eating food that has fallen on the floor, and washing their hands with soap and water before eating meals or snacks and after going to the toilet or handling animals.

Pets should not be allowed near food, dishes, worktops or food preparation areas.

Food safety and hygiene hints

- Do not leave perishable food at room temperatures for more than 2 hours. Perishable food brought from home, including sandwiches, should be kept in a fridge or cool place below 8°C.

- Insulated cool boxes, or a cool box with cool packs, should be used for carrying food when taking children on trips or outings.

- Eggs should be kept in the fridge.

- Eggs given to babies or toddlers should be cooked until both the yolk and the white are solid.

- Food stocks should be rotated and food beyond its use-by date discarded.

- If food is to be eaten warm it should be re-heated until piping hot (70°C) for 2 minutes and then cooled down before serving.

- Avoid keeping food hot for long periods.

- Cool leftover food quickly, cover and refrigerate, ideally within 1-2 hours.

- Do not use unpasteurised milk, or milk-based products such as cheese and yoghurt made from unpasteurised milk. If a parent brings in goat's or sheep's milk for their child, check with the parent if the milk needs to be boiled.

- Root vegetables such as carrots and parsnips should always be peeled and topped and tailed. Fruit and vegetables to be eaten raw should be peeled for very young children, and washed well.

- Whole pieces of nut should not be given to under-5s in case of choking. Ground nuts and chopped nuts can be included in foods for under-5s where appropriate.

- Allergic reactions can be very serious. There should be a careful plan for choosing a safe and nutritious diet for any individual child with a true allergy.

General safety issues

- Children under 5 should never be left alone while they are eating, in case they choke.

- All highchairs should be fitted with a safety harness which should be used at all times when children are in the chairs. Children should never be left unsupervised while in a highchair.

For information on food safety and hygiene issues for infants, see page 43.

Eating patterns and timing of meals and snacks

The eating patterns of many pre-school children are erratic and food faddiness is common. Children at this age become rapidly disgruntled when hungry and are likely to require snacks in between their main mealtimes.

If children in child care are given snacks either at inappropriate times or inadequately, they may be ravenous when picked up by their parents or guardians. They may then fill up with snack foods on the way home, which do not provide the same nutritional benefit as a main meal. Carers and parents or guardians may wish to discuss the most appropriate times for afternoon snacks and tea so that this can be avoided.

Breakfast

Children who are cared for outside the family home may have less time for breakfast at home and may benefit from a meal similar to breakfast with their carer. Breakfast cereals served with milk make an important contribution to daily nutrient intakes. The best breakfast cereals for children are those which do not have sugar added and which are often fortified with minerals and vitamins (particularly iron) – for example corn flakes, crisped rice, puffed wheat or wheat bisks. Higher fibre cereals (such as whole grain or bran cereals) should be given in moderation as they are bulky and may fill children up quickly. Cereals (such as muesli) which contain whole nuts should not be given to the under-5s. Carers should look for breakfast cereals which are low in salt and sugar.

It is important that children have

breakfast. Parents and guardians should work together with carers to ensure that children have breakfast, either at home or when they arrive in child care.

Timing of meals and length of meals

Children need to eat regularly. Carers planning the timing of meals and snacks should ensure that they are spaced out appropriately throughout the day, so that, for example, children do not have a long gap between lunch and tea, or between tea and when they go home.

Some children may eat slowly. It is important to ensure that all children have enough time to eat. In some European countries there is a recommendation for the amount of time that should be allowed for meals in nursery settings which seems to vary between 30 and 45 minutes.[27]

Snacks

Children need nutritious snacks between meals. The best snacks are those without added sugar but which offer a range of other nutrients. A variety of snacks should be offered including fruit, vegetables and any type of bread such as sandwiches, yoghurts, dips and other savoury foods (see *Ideas for nutritious snacks*, below). It is best to avoid giving sweets, sweet biscuits, cakes, sugary or fizzy drinks and dried fruit and fruit juices as snacks on their own: keep these foods and drinks to mealtimes only.

How carers can encourage eating well

To help develop social skills, it is good practice for carers to sit with children when they are eating and (where appropriate and if they can), eat the same foods and drink the same drinks. An encouraging and pleasant environment is important at meals and carers provide an important positive role model.[28] In the same way as carers should not smoke in front of children, they should also set a good example in the foods and drinks they choose for themselves.

A meal is a time for eating but it should also be a time for socialising and learning. Children can learn from the carer about table manners, and can practise their speaking and listening skills. To encourage this, distractions such as television should be avoided during mealtimes. All children should be encouraged to do whatever they can for themselves in terms of eating, to help them develop skills and independence. Encouraging good table manners and social skills around eating are an important part of a child's development.

Language development is fostered when children interact in small groups, and carers should sit and chat with children during meals and snacks. Children also enjoy being involved in meal preparation, table setting and clearing away.

Rewards are often given to children as a way of encouraging good behaviour or if they have done well in a particular task. Rather than giving sweets, chocolates and sweet snacks such as biscuits to reward good behaviour, rewards can be given in the form of smiles and praise ('soft rewards') or as small inexpensive items such as stars, stickers or badges ('hard rewards'). Most children are very happy with soft rewards and enjoy getting praise or attention. Older children are more likely to be influenced by hard rewards but a simple stamp on the hand with washable ink (for example

---

Ideas for nutritious snacks

- Dairy foods such as cheese or plain yoghurt with added fruit

- Fresh fruit such as pears, apple slices, satsumas, banana, seedless grapes, slices of melon, mango, pineapple, kiwi, plums (without stones), or berries such as strawberries and raspberries. Choose fruits in season and those that are grown locally where possible. The fruit from canned fruit in juice can be used in fruit kebabs or added to yoghurt or fromage frais.

- Raw vegetables such as peeled carrots, sweet pepper, tomato, cucumber or celery (all well washed) with dips such as houmous or Greek yoghurt with chives

- Home-made plain popcorn

- Plain biscuits such as crispbreads, oatcakes, breadsticks, cream crackers, matzos, rice waffles, melba toast. Some of these foods can be high in salt, so choose those that have less than 0.5g sodium per 100g where possible

- Any type of bread (use a variety of white, brown, wholemeal, granary or crusty breads, including toast); crumpets, English muffins, bagels, pitta bread or sandwiches. Look for lower-salt (low-sodium) versions where available. Suitable fillings for sandwiches might be meat (for example, cold roast meats, chicken, ham, corned beef, meat paste), cheese, cottage cheese, fish paste, mashed pilchards or sardines, tuna, egg, houmous, roast vegetables, banana, salad or combinations of these.

Ideas for nutritious snacks are also included in the sample menus given in chapter 6.

in the shape of a teddy) will allow the child to see and share their 'reward' with parents and guardians.

There is nothing wrong with giving children sweets occasionally and children will often receive them as tokens of affection or to celebrate special events such as Easter, Chinese New Year or Diwali. It is best to give sweets after a main meal rather than between meals as they will do the least damage to teeth at this time and will not spoil the child's appetite.

Making the most of mealtimes

- Sit with the children during meals and snacks.

- If the carer eats at the same time as children, it is important that what the carer eats and drinks provides a good role model for healthy eating.

- Avoid distractions such as television.

- Do not hurry children as they eat.

- Encourage children to try all the food offered to them.

- Encourage good table manners.

- Do not force children to eat all the food offered.

- Chat to the children during the meal.

- Use the mealtime as an opportunity to provide education about healthy eating.

- Respect the behavioural norms and expectations of specific cultures.

Adapted from Nahikan-Nelms, 1997. [5]

Dealing with food refusal

Periods of fussy eating among under-5s are not unusual. Children should be allowed to make their own food choices. If a child refuses a food or meal, the carer should gently encourage them to eat, but children should never be forced to eat. To minimise food refusal, it is important to ensure that a variety of foods are offered. Toddlers may be wary of trying new food (neophobia) and this may also include rejecting foods that they do normally eat if the foods are served in different shapes and sizes or containers.[29] Some toddlers are more neophobic than others and it has been reported that vegetables, fruit and meat are more likely to be rejected by these children.[30]

If a child refuses a food even after gentle encouragement to eat, remove the food without making a fuss or passing judgement. While it is useful to encourage children to try different foods, it is not good practice to reward children for eating food they do not want (particularly by offering the reward of pudding or a sweet snack). Words of praise and encouragement to try foods and eat a variety of foods may help some children at mealtimes. It may be useful to adopt the approach that a food refused is 'not liked today'. Food fads often do not last more than a couple of weeks and children may, at another time, accept a food that was previously rejected. It is important that a good variety of foods are continually offered.

While it can be distressing for carers (and parents or guardians) to have food they have prepared rejected, keeping your own attitude to eating friendly and relaxed will help children to feel that eating is a pleasurable way

Tips for tackling food refusal

- Gently encourage children to eat but if a child refuses to eat, take away the food without passing judgement.

- Praise children when they eat well.

- Eat with children and make positive comments about the food.

- Give small portions. Seconds can always be given.

- Develop a clear routine of meals and snacks, avoiding drinks and snacks close to mealtimes.

- Offer a variety of tastes and textures at meals.

- Make sure the eating environment is calm and relaxed.

- Involve children in shopping, cooking and planning meals.

to satisfy hunger rather than a battleground.

A child's opinion about what they like and dislike should be respected and it is better not to 'disguise' foods that they have rejected. However, changing the form a food is given in may make the food more acceptable. For example, a child might refuse cooked carrots but enjoy raw ones, or may refuse pasta coated in sauce but prefer the pasta and sauce served separately.

Learning through food

Child care provides the opportunity for children to learn about food, food sources, nutrition, health, the seasons, growing cycles and other people's ways of life. Learning how to choose and enjoy many different nutritious foods in early childhood can provide the foundation for a lifetime of wise food choices.[31] Research suggests that even very young children are ready to learn more about food, nutrition and health than previously thought.[32]

Activities involving food will encourage children both to develop a range of skills and to increase their knowledge of food. They will also give children the opportunity to learn about new and different foods, and foods from a variety of cultures should be included, particularly those

Food-related activities

- Making pictures with food – for example, using dried pasta and pulses, rice, seeds or bay leaves
- Cutting out food pictures from magazines for collages, murals or mobiles
- Food prints: halved small potatoes, carrots, apples or parsnips
- Making a seed ball for the birds
- Papier maché fruit and vegetables
- Growing mustard and cress or sprouting seeds
- Making playdough or salt dough
- Having a pretend café or shop
- Food tasting
- Food smells game – for example spices, vinegar, orange, onion, strong cheese
- Food-related songs and rhymes – for example: Five currant buns, Five little peas in a pea-pod pressed, Mix a pancake, Ten fat sausages.

Carers should positively encourage both boys and girls to participate in all activities, including food-related activities such as cooking.

Resources for encouraging learning through food-related activities can be found in Appendix 5.

represented in the place of child care.

Carers can also involve children in preparing food and laying and clearing tables. This will all contribute to their educational experience.

Listening to children

It is important to listen to, and consult with, the children in childcare settings about the choices of foods on offer. Research has shown that pre-school children often want more choice of food and are pleased to be consulted on menu planning.[33] Carers have an important role in listening to children and helping them learn through example. Examples of how carers can develop their skills in listening and responding to young children around food and food-related activities can be obtained from the National Children's Bureau publication *Listening and Responding to Young Children's Views on Food*.[34]

Involving and listening to parents and guardians

It is important to involve parents or guardians in encouraging healthy eating and to listen to their concerns and ideas. Evidence suggests that in many childcare settings there is a lack of partnership between parents and carers on the practicalities of food provision.[35] It may be that parents and carers lack understanding of the other's role in food provision, with both believing that it is the responsibility of the other to provide the nutritious components of the diet such as fruit and vegetables. A real partnership between carers and

parents and guardians should be fostered to ensure that each has the opportunity to communicate their concerns to the other. This could include:

- Meeting with parents or guardians and making sure they are aware that the carers are committed to providing healthy, varied (and enjoyable) food.
- Making menus available to parents, for example by displaying them on a noticeboard, or where children leave their coats. This will help families to plan a diet which is balanced between the childcare setting and home. Carers could also ask parents for suggestions for menu items.
- Giving parents adequate notice of any changes to meals, food choice or any other aspect of food provision, and allowing them to comment on and discuss the changes before they are introduced.
- Giving parents or guardians clear information each day about what food has been eaten and if their child has eaten well. Even older children may not be accurate in reporting what they have eaten.
- Inviting parents and guardians to share special foods and recipes with carers. Carers should seek advice from parents and guardians if they are serving food which the carers themselves are not familiar with. Such food should not only contain the right ingredients but should look and taste right too.

Carers should ask parents or guardians about any special dietary requirements their child has before the child starts attending the childcare setting. Parents or guardians of children who are on special diets (for example a gluten-free diet) or who have food allergies are responsible for providing the carer with information about the food choices available to their child. Parents or guardians should talk to their GP or health visitor for help and advice. The GP may refer the family to a registered dietitian. In some cases, the carer may want to insist that the parent or guardian provides the child's food, for example for children on vegan diets.

Bringing food from home

In some cases children may bring food from home to eat while they are in child care. It is helpful if the childcare setting has its own nutrition policy (see the example on page 59). This can be given to parents to help them in choosing and preparing food they send from home. It is reasonable to ask that children who bring food from home have similar food choices to the children who may have food provided for them in child care, particularly for snacks. A nutrition policy could request, for example, that children do not bring packets of crisps or confectionery with them. It is advisable to discuss these issues with parents when they are organising their childcare or before changes are introduced.

Food for special occasions

Food is often eaten to celebrate special occasions. For example, sharing a birthday cake may be an important social activity.

Foods given as treats at home to mark special occasions are often based around sweets, cakes and biscuits and there is nothing wrong with the occasional treat. Where a large number of children are cared for together, however, there may be so many birthdays

Some of the most common festivals and celebrations throughout the year

January	1st: New Year
	6th: Epiphany: Three Kings Day
	7th: Rastafarian New Year
	25th: Burns' Night
Late January/early February	Chinese New Year
	Jewish New Year for Trees
February	3rd: Japanese bean scattering
	14th: Valentine's Day
	40 days before Easter: Pancake Day (Shrove Tuesday)
Late February/early March	Caribbean Carnival
	Chinese Festival of Light
	Purim (Jewish)
March	17th: St Patrick's Day
	Baha'i New Year
	Holi (Hindu Harvest Festival)
March/April	Mothering Sunday
	Passover (Jewish festival of Pesach)
	Easter
May	1st: May Day
	Wesak: Buddhist festival, first day of full moon in May
Late May/June	Shavuot: Jewish Festival of Weeks
	Tuan Yang Chieh: Chinese Dragon Boat Festival
August	Raksha Bhandhan: Indian celebration of brotherly/sisterly love
September/early October	Jewish New Year: Yom Kippur
	Chinese Kite Festival
	Harvest Festival
October/November	31st: Halloween
	Diwali: Hindu Festival of Light
November	5th: Guy Fawkes
	Thanksgiving
December	6th: St Nicholas
	Hanukkah (Jewish Festival)
	25th: Christmas Day
	26th: Boxing Day

Festivals such as Eid-ul-Fitr, the Islamic festival of fast-breaking linked to Ramadan, occurs at a different time each year: parents will be able to advise carers on these dates. For a current calendar of religious festivals contact the SHAP Working Party (address on page 86).

and other special occasions (for example Christmas, Easter, Diwali, Eid-ul-Fitr, Halloween, Chinese New Year, or birth of new brothers and sisters) that it is almost a daily event. Carers may therefore wish to think of other special ways of celebrating. The children are also likely to celebrate outside of their child care so are unlikely to miss out on special foods. Decorating the room with balloons and streamers, encouraging children to dress up or wear party hats, playing party games and presenting foods in interesting shapes can make a party without the need for sweets, crisps, biscuits and cakes. A birthday cake made out of play dough with real candles will allow the ritual 'blowing out' of the candles to make the birthday child feel special.

Holidays, festivals and religious occasions of various cultures provide a valuable opportunity to include special occasion food and to involve the parents. The mix of children being cared for will determine which festivals in particular are celebrated, but it is important for children to learn about and celebrate occasions and cultures not represented among them too. These events provide a springboard for all sorts of activities, not just those related to foods, and are an important part of early years learning.

If parents wish to provide special treats for the children to help celebrate these occasions, let them know what your policy is for food for special occasions and festivals so that they know what to send in. Care should be taken when sharing foods that have not been prepared in the childcare setting as the ingredients used will not be known. Carers need to be aware if any of the children in their care have a food allergy, so that they can ensure that these children do not come into contact

with any foods they might be allergic to.

The box on page 58 shows a calendar of many of the main annual events.

Developing a nutrition policy

The best way to make sure that the recommendations and advice about healthy eating are agreed between the carer(s) and parents or guardians is to write a nutrition policy. This is not as difficult to do as it may sound: many childcare settings already have a lot of 'unwritten' rules about food and eating. The advantage of writing them down as a 'policy' is that everyone has a chance to agree these ideas and in addition they provide information to new parents about your approach to healthy eating.

Sample nutrition policy

- The weekly menu will be on display in advance. Recipes will be available to parents.

- The weekly menu will provide children in child care with a tasty, varied diet.

- All the children in child care will have suitable food made available for them.

- Children who do not receive breakfast at home will be offered this when they arrive, if this is agreed with parents or guardians.

- Milk will be served with morning and afternoon snacks.

- Soy milk drinks will only be given as a substitute for cow's milk with the parent's agreement and then only those fortified with calcium will be given.

- Water will be available at all times.

- Diluted fruit juice will be served with the main meal.

- Children will be allowed to have second helpings of fruit or milk-based desserts.

- Children will still receive dessert if they refuse their main course.

- Sweets and soft drinks will not be served.

- Parents or guardians will be advised if their child is not eating well.

- Parents of children who are on special diets will be asked to provide as much information as possible about suitable foods and in some cases may be asked to provide the food themselves.

- A specific allergy plan will be in place to deal with any child having an allergic reaction.

- Carers will sit with children while they eat and will provide a good role model for healthy eating.

- Withholding food will not be used as a form of punishment.

- Children will be encouraged to develop good eating skills and table manners and will be given plenty of time to eat.

- Advice will be given to parents about suitable foods to bring from home.

- Children will be encouraged to play outside every day, weather permitting. This will ensure that they have an opportunity to be exposed to summer sunlight which helps their bodies to make vitamin D.

A nutrition policy should not be seen as something set in stone, but something open to regular review.

A sample nutrition policy is given on page 59 as a guide to the sort of information that you may wish to include.

Healthy eating awards

In some areas of the country, healthy eating awards have been established to encourage better food and drink provision in early years settings. One example of this is the Under-5s Healthy Eating Award set up by Bedfordshire dietitians and oral health promoters. Over 100 childcare settings and 50 childminders have obtained an award which means that they have received appropriate staff training and have met targets on the food served at meals, the social aspects of eating and drinking, food safety and hygiene, dental registration, use of suitable dining and eating equipment, managing celebrations appropriately and liaising with parents. For more information about this scheme, contact dietitians@ldh.nhs.uk.

References

1 Dowler E, Calvert C. 1995. *Nutrition and Diet in Lone Parent Families in London*. London: Family Policy Studies Centre.

2 Kant AK, Schatzkin A, Harris TB, Ziegler RG, Block G. 1993. Dietary diversity and subsequent mortality in the First National Health and Nutrition Examination Survey Epidemiologic Follow-Up Study. *American Journal of Clinical Nutrition;* 57: 434-440.

3 Story M, Brown JE. 1987. Do children instinctively know what to eat? The studies of Clara David revisited. *New England Journal of Medicine;* 316: 103-106.

4 Birch LL, McPhee L, Shoba BC, Pirok E, Steinburg L. 1987. What kind of exposure reduces children's neophobia? *Appetite;* 9: 171-178.

5 Nahikan-Nelms M. 1997. Influential factors in care-giver behaviour at meal-times: a study of 24 child care programs. *Journal of the American Dietetic Association;* 97: 505-509.

6 Gregory JR, Collins DL, Davies PSW, Hughes JM, Clarke PC. 1995. *National Diet and Nutrition Survey: Children Aged 1$^1/_2$ to 4$^1/_2$ Years. Volume 1: Report of the Diet and Nutrition Survey*. London: HMSO.

7 Attree P. 2005. Low-income mothers, nutrition and health: a systematic review of qualitative evidence. *Maternal and Child Nutrition;* 1: 227-240.

8 www.fiveaday.nhs.uk

9 Wardle J, Cook LJ, Gibson EL, Sapochnik M, Sheiham A, Lawson M. 2003. Increasing children's acceptance of vegetables: a randomised trial of parent-led exposure. *Appetite;* 40: 155-162.

10 Department of Health. 2004. *At Least Five a Week. Evidence on the Impact of Physical Activity and its Relationship to Health. A Report from the Chief Medical Officer*. London: Department of Health.

11 Jago R, Baranowski T, Baranowski JC, Thompson D, Greaves KA. 2005. BMI from 3-6 years of age is predicted by TV viewing and physical activity not diet. *International Journal of Obesity;* 29: 557-564.

12 To obtain a copy of *Nursery Milk Guide: For Providers of Day Care for Children Under 5*. (2003), write to: WRFU, PO Box 31048, London SW1V 2FF. Tel: 020 7887 1258.

13 Hourihane JO'B, Rolls CJ. 1995. Morbidity from excessive intakes of high energy fluids: the squash drinking syndrome. *Archives of Disease in Childhood;* 72: 141-143.

14 Watt RG, Dykes J, Sheiham A. 2000. Preschool children's consumption of drinks: implications for dental health. *Community Dental Health;* 17: 8-13.

15 Chestnutt IG, Murdoch C, Robson KF. 2003. Parents' and carers' choice of drinks for infants and toddlers in areas of social and economic disadvantage. *Community Dental Health;* 20: 139-145.

16 Watt RG, Dykes J, Sheiham A. 2000. Drink consumption in British preschool children: relation to vitamin C, iron and calcium intakes. *Journal of Human Nutrition and Dietetics;* 13: 13-19.

17 Hinds K, Gregory J. 1995. *National Diet and Nutrition Survey: Children Aged 1$^1/_2$ to 4$^1/_2$ Years. Volume 2. Report of the Dental Survey*. London: HMSO.

18 Department of Health. 2005. *Children's Dental Health in the United Kingdom* 2003. London: TSO.

19 Harris R, Nicoll AD, Adair PM, Pine CM. 2004. Risk factors for dental caries in young children: a systematic review of the literature. *Community Dental Health*, 21, (1 suppl): 71-85.

20 Moynihan P. 2003. Fruit juice and dried fruit – healthy choices or not? Letter in the *British Dental Journal;* 194: 408.

21 Habibian M, Roberts G, Lawson M, Stevenson R, Harris S. 2001. Dietary habits and dental health over the first 18 months of life. *Community Dentistry and Oral Epidemiology;* 29: 239-246.

22 European Union Directive. 2005. *Processed Cereal-based and Baby-foods for Infants and Young Children Regulations 2004*.

23 Dean T. 1997. Prevalence of allergic disorders in early childhood. *Pediatric Allergy and Immunology;* 8 (suppl 10): 27-31.

24 Department of Health. 1998. *Report on Peanut Allergy. Committee on Toxicity of Chemicals in Food, Consumer Products and the Environment. (COT)*. London: TSO.

25 Food Standards Agency. 2004. Food Labelling Regulations (Amendment No 2). Accessed from www.food.gov.uk/multimedia/pdfs/allergenukg uidance.pdf

26 Bellisle F. 2004. Effects of diet on behaviour and cognition in children. *British Journal of Nutrition;* 92; suppl 2: S227-S232.

27 Children in Europe. 2006. *An Appetite for Life: Young Children, Food and Eating*. Accessed from www.childrenineurope.org

28 Birch LL. 1980. Effects of peer models' food choices and eating behaviours on preschoolers' food preferences. *Child Development;* 51: 489-496.

29 Addessi E, Galloway AT, Visalberghi E, Birch LL. 2005. Specific social influences on the acceptance of novel foods in 2-5 year old children. *Appetite;* 45: 264-271.

30 Cooke L, Wardle J, Gibson EL. 2003. Relationship between parental report of neophobia and everyday food consumption in 2-6 year old children. *Appetite;* 41: 205-206.

31 Singleton JC, Achterburg CL, Shannon B. 1992. The role of food and nutrition in the health perceptions of young children. *Journal of the American Dietetic Association;* 92: 67-70.

32 Anliker JA, Laus MJ, Sammonds KW, Beal VA. 1990. Parental messages and the nutrition awareness of preschool children. *Journal of Nutrition Education;* 22: 24-29.

33 Mooney A, Blackburn T. 2003. *Children's Views on Childcare Quality*. London: Department for Education and Skills.

34 McAuliffe AM, Lane J. 2005. *Listening and Responding to Young Children's Views on Food*. London: National Children's Bureau.

35 Moore H, Nelson P, Marshall J, Cooper M, Zambas H, et al. 2005. Laying foundations for health: Food provision for under 5's in day care. *Appetite;* 44: 207-213.

Chapter 6
Nutritional guidelines and menu planning

In this chapter, recommendations – in the form of 'nutrient-based standards' – are made for the amount of energy and nutrients, and some foods, that should typically be provided for a group of children aged under 5 who receive meals and snacks in child care or other early years settings. This chapter also gives some recommendations for menu planners on how to put together varied and interesting menus, and shows three examples of menus which meet the nutrient-based standards.

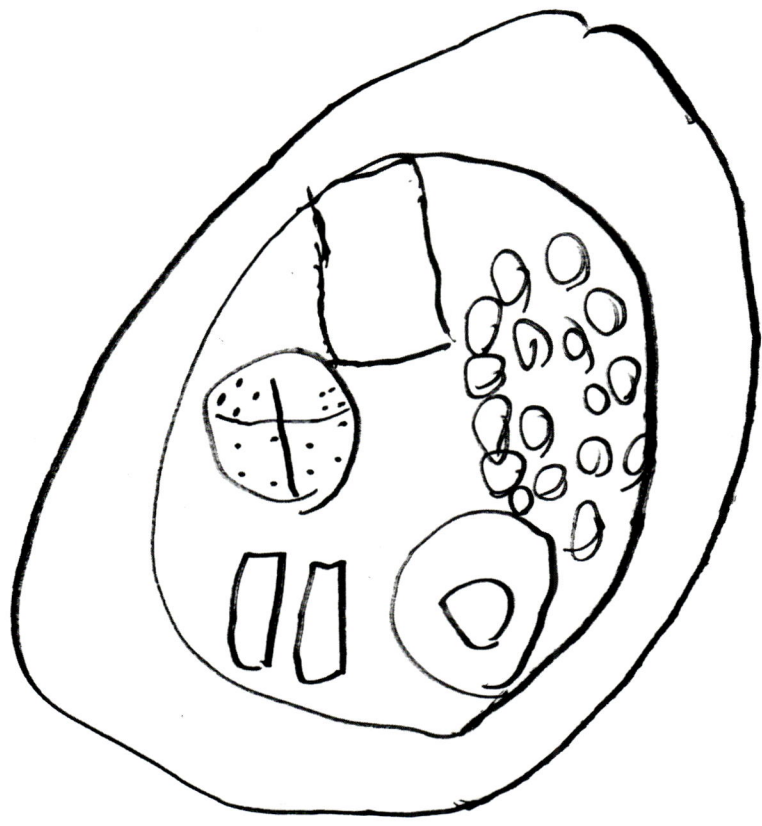

Eggs, peas, bread and carrots
Imogen, aged 4

Why nutrient-based standards are the most effective way to improve menu planning

Nutrient-based standards specify the amounts of nutrients, and some foods, that should be provided to a group of people over a period of time to ensure that the nutritional needs of everyone in that group are met. They are based on the *Dietary Reference Values for Food Energy and Nutrients for the UK*[1] and other appropriate guidance which aims to promote good health through good food and drink choices. Nutrient-based standards provide a numerical but flexible framework to help menu planners put together varied menus that are suitable for the people they serve.

To use nutrient-based standards effectively requires simple tools which can also act as a training tool for those who plan menus or provide food for others. The Caroline Walker Trust produced a computerised menu planner tool in 2001 (CHOMP) which allowed menu planners to put together, easily and quickly, menus which meet nutrient-based standards for under-5s from a detailed database of foods and drinks. This has been extensively used in the early years sector and evaluation has suggested that using nutrient-based standards is neither onerous nor complicated for providers if appropriate tools are provided. A new updated computer tool to work with the standards for under-5s in this report is currently being produced and details can be found on the Caroline Walker Trust website www.cwt.org.uk.

Menu planners should ensure that any menu analysis software they use is based on nutrient values for cooked foods and recipes and that, where the software has not been specially prepared for planning menus for under-5s, necessary help with analysis is provided by a registered dietitian or registered public health nutritionist.

Adopting nutrient-based standards, and providing the necessary tools and support for those who provide food for under-5s in the UK, sends a clear message that policy makers take the promotion of good nutrition seriously.

Nutrient-based standards encourage transparency among all stakeholders as the composition of foods, recipes and ingredients used in menus are clear and confusions that can arise from food-based standards between similar food products are avoided. Nutrient-based standards also allow good practice to be shared and make it possible to monitor the implementation of standards and carry out an on-going evaluation of how standards are being met and where extra support is needed.

In addition, adopting nutrient-based standards, and providing the necessary tools and support for those who provide food for under-5s in the UK, sends a clear message that policy makers take the promotion of good nutrition seriously.

All those who inspect childcare services in the UK should monitor the nutritional standards of the food served in the childcare and other early years settings they visit. Inspectors' reports should include comments on food and nutrition. Any childcare setting that does not meet the standards should seek advice from a registered dietitian or registered public health nutritionist.

How the nutrient-based standards have been calculated

Children have different needs depending on their age and gender, and the requirements of every child will be different. The recommendations therefore represent average intakes. If the food offered to a group of children provides the amount of nutrients recommended, and the children receive the balance of their requirements at home, then the nutritional needs of most members of that group are likely to be met. The recommendations are not designed for individuals but act as a framework for menu planners and those advising menu planners on appropriate diets.

The recommendations are based on percentages of the total daily intake of nutrients required by an 'average' child in a group of 1-4 year olds, or a group of 1-2 year olds, or a group of 3-4 year olds. Children will spend different periods of time in child care and the recommendations consider the needs of:

- **1-4 year olds** in full-day or half-day child care, or for those having individual meals and snacks while in child care
- **1-2 year olds** in full-day or half-day child care, or for those

having individual meals and snacks while in child care, and

- **3-4 year olds** in full-day or half-day child care, or for those having individual meals and snacks while in child care.

It is recommended that the food provided in full-day child care should give children 70% of their requirements for energy and most other nutrients.

The recommendations apply to children who attend all forms of child care including playgroups, nursery units and reception classes, and are based on average Dietary Reference Values for boys and girls.

The derived nutrient values from which the nutrient-based standards have been calculated are given on page 82.

Standards for particular nutrients

Fat

The current advice for adults and children over 5 years is to consume a diet in which about 35% of their daily energy needs are provided by the fat in food and added to food. It has generally been suggested that the fat intake of children aged under 2 years should not be restricted, as the under-2s need foods which are energy-dense and nutrient-dense – that is, foods which pack a lot of calories and other nutrients into a small amount of food. However, evidence from a large longitudinal study of children at 18 months suggests that there is no evidence that children who get 30-35% of their energy from fat experience delayed growth, and there is in fact evidence that children who get 39-43% of their energy from fat may have lower intakes of iron and vitamin C and lower iron status.[2] It has also been reported that higher fat intakes are associated with higher total cholesterol levels among boys even at this young age and this again may suggest that moderate fat intakes among under-5s may be beneficial for future health. The Caroline Walker Trust therefore recommends that about 35% of food energy in the diets of under-5s should typically come from fat – about the same proportion as for the population as a whole. No specific recommendations are made about saturated fat for under-5s, however, since recommendations made for adults are inappropriate for the under-5s who still have a relatively high milk consumption.

While it is important that children who have poor appetites or who are fussy eaters get enough food that they will accept to ensure their healthy growth and development, evidence also suggests that the best sources of energy for under-5s are – as they are for adults – starchy carbohydrate foods. However, under-5s should not be given low-fat foods designed for adults (with the exception of semi-skimmed milk – see page 47). Nor should they have diets that are very bulky and high in fibre which may mean they find it difficult to eat enough calories for their needs. For more information about fat in the diet, see page 21.

Iron

The iron intake of children under 5 is lower than currently recommended and there is evidence to suggest that low iron status is common in this age group (see page 32). For this reason, the Caroline Walker Trust recommends that the intakes of iron in the diet of children in full-day child care should be enhanced to provide not less than 80% of the Reference Nutrient Intake, and proportionately more for half-day care as described in the tables on pages 65-68. Iron

will be provided in particular by main meals. Drinks (including milk) and many snacks are likely to be low in iron, so it is important that children receive the bulk of their iron from their meals. Good sources of iron are shown in Appendix 2 and more information about iron in the diet and improving iron status is given on page 32.

Care needs to be taken when planning menus for children receiving a vegetarian diet to ensure they obtain sufficient iron. For more information about vegetarian diets, see page 51.

Zinc

Low intakes of zinc have been reported among a large proportion of under-5s – particularly when milk intakes start to decline – and it is important that good sources of zinc such as meat and meat dishes, cereals, milk and milk products and eggs are included in the diet regularly (see page 34). Since the majority of zinc is likely to come from foods served at meals, the Caroline Walker Trust recommends that the intakes of zinc for children in full-day child care be enhanced to provide not less than 80% of the Reference Nutrient Intake, as for iron above. Good sources of zinc are shown in Appendix 2.

Salt

New guidance on target average salt intakes for children have been set by the Scientific Advisory Committee on Nutrition (SACN)[3] (see page 35). It is suggested that children aged 1-3 years should have no more than 2g of salt per day and children 4-5 years no more than 3g of salt per day. The maximum recommended amount of salt for groups of 1-4 year olds, 1-2 year olds and 3-4 year olds used in this report are given in Appendix

3. These figures have been included in the nutrient-based standards but it will be difficult to achieve them. Currently many commonly consumed foods such as bread, biscuits, breakfast cereals, cheese, meat and fish products and tinned foods are high in salt and we do not want to exclude some of these foods as they may offer other useful nutrients. It is possible to achieve the salt recommendations if predominantly home-cooked foods are used, but some flexibility is needed when planning menus, to ensure that caterers are still able to serve a good variety of foods that children like. Manufacturers and retailers are making changes to the salt content of many commonly consumed foods and therefore over time it may become easier to meet the salt recommendations.

Vitamin D

There is a UK reference value for vitamin D for children aged 6 months to 3 years of 7 micrograms a day. For children aged 4 years and above there is an assumption that they will make enough vitamin D through the action of sunlight on their skin. As explained on page 28, there is increasing concern that many pre-school children have low vitamin D status and parents are recommended to continue giving vitamin D supplementation (through vitamin drops) until their child's fifth birthday. It is difficult for children to obtain the recommended amount of vitamin D from food alone since there are few good food sources of vitamin D (see Appendix 2). Vitamin D is not included in the nutrient-based standards on pages 65-68 but there is additional information on page 71 on how to ensure that menus are rich in vitamin D.

Standards for different periods of time spent in child care

Children in full-day child care (8 hours or more)

Children in child care for a full day will receive the majority of their food while in child care and therefore it is recommended that the food provided gives the children 70% of their daily requirement for energy and most other nutrients, and no more than 70% of the maximum recommended amount of non-milk extrinsic sugars and sodium/salt. The remaining 30% of energy and other nutrients will come from breakfast and from any drinks, snacks or light meals the child receives at home. Children in child care for a whole day should receive not less than 80% of their requirements for iron and zinc, since the diets of some children under the age of 5 are low in these nutrients.

All children are encouraged to have breakfast. This could either be at home or in child care. Fortified breakfast cereals in particular provide a valuable source of some important vitamins and minerals. Parents and guardians and those providing child care should work together to ensure that children have breakfast either at home or in child care. The recommendations for daily intakes of nutrients do not include the contribution made by breakfast.

Children in half-day care

Half-day care involves either a morning or afternoon session and is likely to include one meal and at least one snack. Lunch is likely to be the major provider of food during the day and therefore children who have lunch and a snack should receive 40% of their daily requirement for energy and at least 40% of their daily needs for most nutrients (and no more than 40% of the recommended maximum amount of non-milk extrinsic sugars or sodium/salt) from these meals, and not less than 45% for iron and zinc. Those having a snack and tea should receive not less than 30% of their needs (and not less than 35% for iron and zinc).

Children having a snack only

Children in child care for a morning or afternoon session which does not include a meal should receive a snack during this session if the period of care exceeds 2 hours. They should have two snacks if the session is 5 hours or more but does not include a meal – for example 12.30pm to 5.30pm care, missing lunch and leaving before tea.

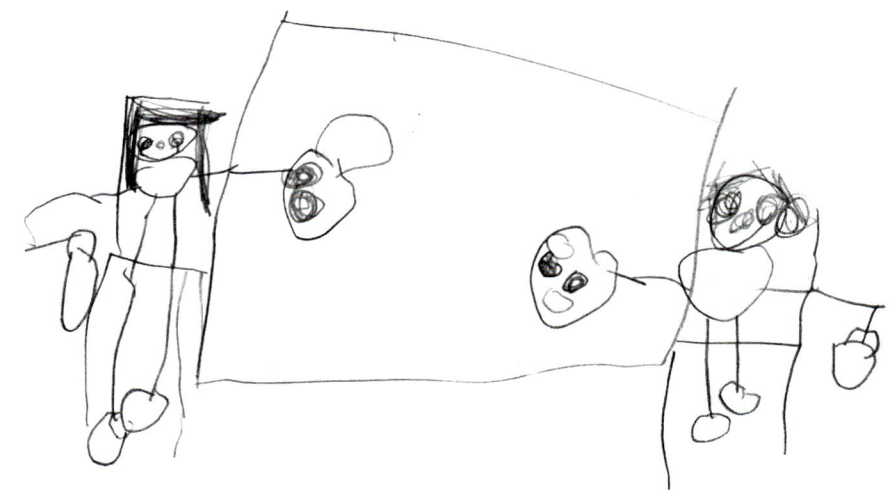

Aidan and me at the table eating cucumber and tomatoes
Eva, aged 4

Nutrient-based standards for food prepared for 1-4 YEAR OLDS in child care: SUMMARY OF RECOMMENDATIONS

The table below summarises the proportion of nutrients that each eating occasion should achieve for children in child care. The figures are for the recommended average nutrient content of meals and snacks provided for children over a one-week period.

Nutrient		FULL-DAY CARE *	Morning session: SNACK and LUNCH	Afternoon session: SNACK and TEA	SNACK only	LUNCH only	TEA only
Energy % of the Estimated Average Requirement (EAR)		70%	40%	30%	10%	30%	20%
Fat % of food energy		About 35%	About 35%	About 35%	About 35%	About 35%	About 35%
Total carbohydrate % of food energy		About 50%	About 50%	About 50%	About 50%	About 50%	About 50%
Non-milk extrinsic sugars % of food energy	MAX	11%	11%	11%	11%	11%	11%
Protein % of the Reference Nutrient Intake (RNI)	MIN	70%	40%	30%	10%	30%	20%
Iron % of the RNI	MIN	80%	45%	35%	10%	35%	25%
Zinc % of the RNI	MIN	80%	45%	35%	10%	35%	25%
Calcium % of the RNI	MIN	70%	40%	30%	10%	30%	20%
Vitamin A % of the RNI	MIN	70%	40%	30%	10%	30%	20%
Vitamin C % of the RNI	MIN	70%	40%	30%	10%	30%	20%
Sodium % of the SACN target average	MAX	70%	40%	30%	10%	30%	20%
Salt % of the SACN target average	MAX	70%	40%	30%	10%	30%	20%
Fruit and vegetables		Aim to offer 4-5 different types.	During the day carers should offer children 4-5 different types of fruits and vegetables at meals and snacks.				

* Full-day care includes a morning snack, lunch, afternoon snack and tea. It does not include breakfast.

% of food energy = Percentage of calories consumed
EAR = Estimated Average Requirement
RNI = Reference Nutrient Intake
SACN = Scientific Advisory Committee on Nutrition[3]
For an explanation of these terms see page 81.

How do the standards translate into specific nutrients for groups of children of different ages?

The tables below and on pages 67-68 show what the nutrient-based standards mean in terms of nutrients and foods for groups of children of different ages.

Nutrient-based standards for food prepared for 1-4 YEAR OLDS in child care

This table provides figures for the recommended nutrient content of an average day's food and drink over a period of one week or more.

Nutrient			FULL-DAY CARE *	Morning session: SNACK and LUNCH	Afternoon session: SNACK and TEA	SNACK only	LUNCH only	TEA only
Energy		kcals	903	516	387	129	387	258
Fat		g	35.0	20.0	15.0	5.0	15.0	10.0
Total carbohydrate		g	120.4	68.8	51.6	17.2	51.6	34.4
Non-milk extrinsic sugars	MAX	g	26.6	15.2	11.4	3.8	11.4	7.6
Protein	MIN	g	11.0	6.3	4.7	1.6	4.7	3.1
Iron	MIN	mg	5.5	3.1	2.4	0.7	2.4	1.7
Zinc	MIN	mg	4.3	2.4	1.9	0.5	1.9	1.4
Calcium	MIN	mg	260	150	110	40	110	70
Vitamin A	MIN	µg	300	170	130	40	130	90
Vitamin C	MIN	mg	21	12	9	3	9	6
Sodium	MAX	mg	630	360	270	90	270	180
Salt	MAX	g	1.6	0.9	0.7	0.2	0.7	0.5
Fruit and vegetables			Aim to offer 4-5 different types.	During the day carers should offer children 4-5 different types of fruits and vegetables at meals and snacks.				

Drinking water should be available throughout the day.

Numbers have been rounded up or down where necessary, to ensure that figures for different periods of child care add up appropriately.

* Full-day care includes a morning snack, lunch, afternoon snack and tea. It does not include breakfast.

Nutrient-based standards for food prepared for 1-2 YEAR OLDS in child care

This table provides figures for the recommended nutrient content of an average day's food and drink over a period of one week or more.

Nutrient			FULL-DAY CARE *	Morning session: SNACK and LUNCH	Afternoon session: SNACK and TEA	SNACK only	LUNCH only	TEA only
Energy		kcals	770	440	330	110	330	220
Fat		g	30.0	17.1	12.8	4.3	12.8	8.5
Total carbohydrate		g	102.7	58.7	44.0	14.7	44.0	29.3
Non-milk extrinsic sugars	MAX	g	22.6	12.9	9.7	3.2	9.7	6.5
Protein	MIN	g	10.2	5.9	4.4	1.5	4.4	2.9
Iron	MIN	mg	5.5	3.1	2.4	0.7	2.4	1.7
Zinc	MIN	mg	4.0	2.3	1.8	0.5	1.8	1.3
Calcium	MIN	mg	245	140	105	35	105	70
Vitamin A	MIN	µg	280	160	120	40	120	80
Vitamin C	MIN	mg	21	12	9	3	9	6
Sodium	MAX	mg	560	320	240	80	240	160
Salt	MAX	g	1.4	0.8	0.6	0.2	0.6	0.4
Fruit and vegetables			Aim to offer 4-5 different types.	During the day carers should offer children 4-5 different types of fruits and vegetables at meals and snacks.				

Drinking water should be available throughout the day.

Numbers have been rounded up or down where necessary, to ensure that figures for different periods of child care add up appropriately.

* Full-day care includes a morning snack, lunch, afternoon snack and tea. It does not include breakfast.

Nutrient-based standards for food prepared for 3-4 YEAR OLDS in child care

This table provides figures for the recommended nutrient content of an average day's food and drink over a period of one week or more.

Nutrient			FULL-DAY CARE *	Morning session: SNACK and LUNCH	Afternoon session: SNACK and TEA	SNACK only	LUNCH only	TEA only
Energy		kcals	1,036	592	444	148	444	296
Fat		g	40.3	23.0	17.3	5.7	17.3	11.6
Total carbohydrate		g	138.1	78.9	59.2	19.7	59.2	39.5
Non-milk extrinsic sugars	MAX	g	30.3	17.3	13.0	4.3	13.0	8.7
Protein	MIN	g	11.9	6.8	5.1	1.7	5.1	3.4
Iron	MIN	mg	5.3	3.0	2.3	0.7	2.3	1.6
Zinc	MIN	mg	4.6	2.6	2.0	0.6	2.0	1.4
Calcium	MIN	mg	280	160	120	40	120	80
Vitamin A	MIN	µg	315	180	135	45	135	90
Vitamin C	MIN	mg	21	12	9	3	9	6
Sodium	MAX	mg	700	400	300	100	300	200
Salt	MAX	g	1.75	1.0	0.75	0.25	0.75	0.5
Fruit and vegetables			Aim to offer 4-5 different types.	During the day carers should offer children 4-5 different types of fruits and vegetables at meals and snacks.				

Drinking water should be available throughout the day.

Numbers have been rounded up or down where necessary, to ensure that figures for different periods of child care add up appropriately.

* Full-day care includes a morning snack, lunch, afternoon snack and tea. It does not include breakfast.

Recommendations for menu planners

In order to help those planning menus to provide a good variety of foods in the proportions that are likely to ensure that all the nutrient needs are met, some simple food-based recommendations for 1-4 year olds in childcare settings are included here.

Food group	How much to serve?	Good choices	Notes
STARCHY FOODS Bread, other cereals and potatoes	Foods from this group should be offered at every meal, and can be useful foods to offer as part of snacks. These foods should make up about a third of the food served each day.	All types of **bread** – wholemeal, granary, brown, wheatgerm, white, multigrain, soda bread, potato bread, chapatis, naan bread, rotis, rolls, bagels, pitta bread, wraps, tortilla	Look for lower-salt breads.
		Potatoes or sweet potatoes – boiled, mashed, baked or wedges	Processed potato products like waffles or smiley faces should be avoided.
		Yam, plaintain, cocoyam, cassava and other starchy root vegetables	
		Pasta and noodles – wholemeal and white	Avoid dried or canned ready-prepared pasta in sauce as these are very salty.
		Rice – brown and white rice	Avoid fried rice or flavoured dried rice in packets.
		Other grains such as couscous or bulgur wheat, maize (polenta) and cornmeal	
		Breakfast cereals – low-sugar, low-salt cereals such as porridge, puffed wheat, wheat bisks, crisped rice or flaked wheat. Fortified cereals can be a good source of iron.	Avoid sugary breakfast cereals. (If a food contains more than 10g of sugar per 100g, it is considered a high-sugar food.)
FRUIT AND VEGETABLES	Offer different fruits and vegetables at meals and snacks. Aim for each day's menu for childcare settings to offer: **1-2 types of fruit** and **2-3 types of vegetables.** Children in full-day care should have the opportunity to try 4-5 different fruits and vegetables each day.	All types of **fresh, frozen and canned vegetables** – for example, broccoli, Brussels sprouts, cabbage, carrots, cauliflower, mushrooms, parsnips, peas, peppers, spinach, swede, sweet potato, turnip	Avoid vegetables canned with added salt and sugar. Do not overcook fresh vegetables, or cut them up a long time before cooking and leave them in water, or cook them early and re-heat before serving – these practices all reduce the vitamin content.
		All types of **salad vegetables** – for example, lettuce, watercress, cucumber, tomato, raw carrot, raw pepper, radish or beetroot	
		All types of **fresh fruit** – such as apples, bananas, pears, grapes, kiwi fruit, oranges, plums, berries, melon or mango	
		All types of **canned fruit in juice** – for example, peaches, pears, pineapple, mandarin oranges, prunes, guava or lychees	
		Stewed fruit such as stewed apple, stewed dried fruit, stewed plums, stewed currants or stewed rhubarb	Sugar can be added to sweeten very sour fruit.
		Dried fruit such as raisins, dried apricots, dates, dried figs, prunes	Avoid dried fruit with added sugar and vegetable oil. Serve dried fruit with meals and not as snacks.

Food group	How much to serve?	Good choices	Notes
MILK AND MILK PRODUCTS Milk, cheese and yoghurt	Foods from this group should be offered at 2-3 meals and snacks each day.	**Milk** – Whole milk should be served for under-2s. Over-2s can have semi-skimmed milk if they are good eaters.	Avoid unpasteurised milk and milk drinks with added sugar.
		Cheese	Avoid unpasteurised cheese and mould-ripened (blue-vein) cheeses. Vegetarian cheese should be used where appropriate.
		Yoghurt and fromage frais	Avoid yoghurts and fromage frais that have a high sugar content (often those with added bits or mousse style). If the sugar content on a yoghurt or fromage frais label says it has more than 15g of sugar per 100g, it is a high sugar option. It is preferable to add fresh fruit to natural yoghurt or fromage frais.
MEAT, FISH and ALTERNATIVES	Main meals should always contain an item from this group. Foods in this group are high in iron and can also be usefully served as part of snacks – for example in sandwich fillings.	**Meat** – all types including beef, lamb, pork, chicken and turkey	Avoid processed meat products which are high in fat and salt, such as crumb-coated chicken products, burgers, pies and canned meats. Some meat products such as sausages are popular with under-5s. Choose good quality versions if you serve these foods, and serve them no more than once a week.
		Fish includes: • **white fish** such as cod, haddock, coley and white fish varieties from sustainable fish stocks such as pollack, saithe and blue whiting • **oil-rich fish** such as herring and mackerel, salmon, trout, sardines, sprats or pilchards. Canned tuna does not count as an oil-rich fish but is a good source of nutrients.	If you are buying fish from a supermarket, look for the blue and white logo of the Marine Stewardship Council, which guarantees sustainability. Serve processed fish products such as fish fingers or fish bites no more than once a week. Make sure fish dishes are free of bones.
		Eggs – including boiled, scrambled or poached, or in an omelette	All eggs should be well cooked.
		Pulses – including all sorts of beans and peas such as butter beans, kidney beans, chick peas, lentils, processed peas or baked beans	Look for canned pulses with no added salt and sugar. Dahl and other dishes made from pulses should be made without adding a lot of oil and salt. Choose lower-salt and low-sugar baked beans.
		Meat alternatives – such as soya mince, textured vegetable protein, quorn or tofu	Processed products made from meat alternatives (eg. vegetarian sausages, burgers and pies) can be high in fat or salt and should not be served more than once in a week.

To increase the amount of dietary VITAMIN D in menus served in child care

- Use margarine fortified with vitamin D for baking and as a fat spread.
- Include an oil-rich fish that is rich in vitamin D in the menu at least once a week – for example, herring, mackerel, pilchards, salmon, sardines, trout or roe. These fish contain between 5-14 micrograms of vitamin D per 100g.
- Canned tuna fish can also make a significant contribution to vitamin D intake as it contains about 3.6 micrograms of vitamin D per 100g.
- Egg yolks are rich in vitamin D and eggs contain about 2.0 micrograms of vitamin D per 100g.
- Meat and poultry contribute small but significant amounts of vitamin D.

General menu planning tips

Planning menus ahead will ensure that the best food choices are made and that meals are varied. When choosing meals to include in menus, remember that:

- A variety of foods should be served throughout the menu cycle and a minimum cycle of three weeks is suggested.
- Choose combinations of colours to make the food attractive. Three or four defined areas of colour look good on a plate.
- A combination of different textures increases appeal. Children will appreciate crisp, crunchy, chewy, smooth and soft foods.
- Taste should be varied but meals containing too many different or new flavours may not be acceptable to children.
- Some finger foods as well as foods which require cutlery allow variation at mealtimes.

Sustainability

Concerns about the environmental impact of food travelling long distances, intensive farming and dwindling stocks of some types of fish have prompted Government and many local authorities to encourage more sustainable procurement policies for the buying of food. Those responsible for buying food should attempt to buy food that is grown locally and that is in season. They should also consider purchasing fish with the Marine Stewardship Council logo which ensures it is from a sustainable source. Carers can encourage children to find out more about the food they eat and to make links between food, seasons, agriculture and the environment. For information about sustainable food and educational resources related to food and the environment, see www.soilassociation.org/foodforlife

Sample menus

Below and on pages 73-74 there are three sample menus which meet the nutrient-based standards for a group of children aged 1-4 years in child care for a full day. Younger children will eat smaller portions and older children will require, and want, larger portions at meals and snacks, as will children who do not drink milk.

- Menu 1 is a sample menu for a one-week period. The foods and drinks in this menu provide the recommended amounts of energy and nutrients for children in child care for a full day. Children in half-day care having lunch and a snack would get the recommended amounts by having the mid-morning snacks and lunches shown on the menu. Children in half-day care having a snack and a tea would get the recommended amounts by having the mid-afternoon snacks and teas shown on the menu. Children having the snacks only would achieve the recommendations for snacks.

- Menu 2 is a sample one-week menu which would be suitable for vegetarian children.

- Menu 3 is a sample one-week menu which includes a variety of multicultural dishes.

For more information on these menus – including the portion sizes or weights of the items on the menu, and the recipes for the dishes shown – and additional information on menu planning, see the *Eating Well for Under-5s in Child Care: Training Materials* (details on page 85).

Menu 1: An example menu for 1-4 year olds in child care

	Monday	Tuesday	Wednesday	Thursday	Friday
Mid-morning snack eg. at 10.00am	Milk Canned peaches in juice Whole milk yoghurt	Milk Tabbouleh Breadsticks Cherry tomatoes	Milk Vanilla yoghurt with banana	Milk Finger food selection of: sliced grapes, celery and red pepper	Milk Wholemeal savoury pancakes with butter Apple chunks
Lunch eg. at 12.00-1.00pm Water and diluted fruit juice available	Chicken korma Brown rice Naan bread Fresh fruit salad	Lamb burgers Bubble and squeak Rice pudding with sultanas	Sardines on toast Sliced tomato Milk jelly with mandarins	Vegetable lasagne Mixed salad Stewed apples with custard	Cottage pie Peas Broccoli Rhubarb crumble
Mid-afternoon snack eg. at 3.00pm	Milk Cucumber and carrot sticks Pitta bread Mint and cucumber dip	Milk Popcorn Sliced pear	Milk Wholemeal toast fingers with margarine Apple	Milk Paprika potato wedges Cheese chunks Orange	Milk Fromage frais with pineapple
Tea eg. at 5.00pm Water and diluted fruit juice available	Egg and cress sandwiches Lettuce Cherry tomatoes Banana custard	Tuna and sweetcorn pasta Cucumber Red pepper Fromage frais Satsuma	Savoury omelette Baby jacket potatoes Semolina with pears	Baked beans and white toast squares Yoghurt with dates	Chicken and vegetable couscous Salad Fresh fruit jelly

Drinking water should be available throughout the day.

Menu 2: An example vegetarian menu for 1-4 year olds in child care

	Monday	Tuesday	Wednesday	Thursday	Friday
Mid-morning snack eg. at 10.00am	Milk Breadsticks Houmous dip Cherry tomatoes	Milk Wholemeal savoury pancakes with butter Celery sticks	Milk Apple chunks and sliced grapes	Milk Yoghurt with sliced banana	Milk Wholemeal toast fingers with soft cheese Carrot sticks
Lunch eg. at 12.00-1.00pm Water and diluted fruit juice available	Vegetarian bolognese with wholemeal spaghetti Semolina pudding with dates	Stuffed peppers Potato salad Beansprout and cherry tomato salad Banana custard	Broccoli quiche Mashed potato Baked beans Stewed fruit with Greek yoghurt	Chickpea fritters Sweet potato Sweetcorn Green beans Milk jelly with mandarin oranges	Mixed bean casserole New potatoes Petits pois Swede Fresh fruit salad
Mid-afternoon snack eg. at 3.00pm	Milk Cucumber and carrot sticks Cream crackers with soft cheese	Milk Fromage frais with canned peach	Milk Breadsticks with mint and cucumber dip Kiwi	Milk Popcorn Apple chunks	Milk Mini bowl of curried rice salad Sliced yellow and orange pepper
Tea eg. at 5.00pm Water and diluted fruit juice available	Egg and cress sandwiches Lettuce Fruit flan	Wholemeal pasta twirls Chickpea salad Cucumber and carrot sticks Greek yoghurt with orange	Vegetable couscous Mixed salad Homemade coleslaw Rice pudding with sultanas	Baby jacket potatoes with ratatouille sauce Oaty fruit crumble with custard	Quorn burger in a bun Lettuce and tomato Orange and lemon rice

Drinking water should be available throughout the day.

Cost factors

Healthy eating need not be expensive. The amount of money available will have some influence on food choice but cost considerations should not be allowed to override the importance of providing a healthy and varied diet. Some examples of ways to 'buy wisely' are given below.

- Offer pasta, rice and bread. All bread is a good source of nutrients. Some white breads and soft grain breads have extra nutrients added. Information is given on the label.
- Use vegetables and fruit seasonally.

- If fresh fruit and vegetables are expensive or not available at certain times of the year, use tinned or frozen ones (but check that tinned vegetables have no added salt or sugar).
- Lean meat is often better value than cheaper, fattier varieties.
- Pulses, eggs and tinned fish are economical.

Spending money on cakes, biscuits, squashes and other soft drinks gives poor nutritional value. These foods provide energy but few nutrients and may fill children up between meals with the result that they may not eat enough at mealtimes.

Menu 3: An example menu for 1-4 year olds including some multicultural choices

	Monday	Tuesday	Wednesday	Thursday	Friday
Mid-morning snack eg. at 10.00am	Milk Wholemeal toast with soft cheese Grape slices	Milk Natural yoghurt with banana slices	Milk Wholemeal savoury pancakes with butter Canned peaches	Milk Mini white bread fingers with tuna pâté Apple chunks	Milk Fromage frais Pineapple chunks
Lunch eg. at 12.00-1.00pm Water and diluted fruit juice available	Coconut fish curry Basmati rice Tomato salad Stewed fruit Whole milk yoghurt	Chicken fajitas Sweetcorn salsa Mixed salad Lemon sorbet with wafers	Sweet and sour pork Egg noodles Stir-fried vegetables Chinese fruit salad	Channa aloo Masoor dahl Mixed vegetable pilau Neapolitan ice cream	Chilli con carne Jacket potato with crème fraîche Sliced tomato and watercress salad Banana custard
Mid-afternoon snack eg. at 3.00pm	Milk Cucumber and carrot sticks Pitta bread fingers Houmous dip	Milk Celery, grapes and red pepper platter	Milk Popcorn Lychees	Milk Raita Breadsticks Clementine	Milk Paprika potato wedges Tomato and sweetcorn salsa
Tea eg. at 5.00pm Water and diluted fruit juice available	Spicy ratatouille with tofu Flat bread Watermelon	Savoury omelette Potato dice Cucumber, red pepper and spring onion Fruit smoothies Chewy cereal bar	Fruity couscous Mixed salad Fromage frais with dates	Chapati Chickpea salad Cucumber and carrot stick garnish Spiced banana crumble	Chicken tikka Tortilla strips or wrap Mixed salad Rice pudding with mandarins

Drinking water should be available throughout the day.

Further details of the foods, recipes and portion sizes used in these menus can be found in *Eating Well for Under-5s in Child Care: Training Materials* (see below).

For more information and advice on menu planning

- Additional information on foods and recipes for this age group can be found in the Caroline Walker Trust's *Eating Well for Under-5s in Child Care: Training Materials*. These training materials also contain a CD-ROM providing lots of useful information about foods, recipes and menu planning. This can be obtained from www.cwt.org.uk.

- General information about good choices to make (for example, for snacks or breakfast) is included in chapter 5. Appendix 2 gives a list of good sources of nutrients.

- For other useful sources of information about eating well for the early years, see Appendix 5.

References

1 Department of Health. 1991. *Dietary Reference Values for Food Energy and Nutrients for the United Kingdom. Report on Health and Social Subjects No. 41*. London: HMSO.

2 Rogers J, Emmett P and the ALSPAC Study Team. 2002. Fat content of the diet among pre-school children in Britain: relationship with food and nutrient intakes. *European Journal of Clinical Nutrition;* 56: 252-263.

3 Scientific Advisory Committee on Nutrition. 2003. *Salt and Health*. London: TSO.

National Standards for Childcare

The National Standards for Childcare represent a baseline of quality which no provider in England may fall below. There are national standards for five types of child care:

- full-day care
- sessional care
- crèches
- out-of-school care
- childminders.

The full standards can be obtained from www.ofsted.gov.uk or from DfES publications, PO Box 5050, Sherwood Park, Annesley, Nottingham NG15 0DJ. T: 0845 602 2260 (ref: DfES 0486/2001). National Care Standards for Scotland, published in 2002, can be found at www.scotland.gov.uk/library5/education/ncsee.pdf. National Care Standards for Wales, published in 2000, can be found at www.csiw.wales.gov.uk

A number of standards are relevant to nutritional health (including Standard 7: Health), but only standard 8 is summarised on the right, taken from standards for full-day care. (The equivalent standards for standard 8 for the other childcare options are similar to those shown in this Appendix.)

Standard 8 Food and drink

Children are provided with regular drinks and food in adequate quantities for their needs. Food and drink is properly prepared, nutritious and complies with dietary and religious requirements.

The focus for standard 8

Adequate and nutritious food and drink are essential for children's well being. The registered person and staff have a good understanding of children's dietary and religious requirements and meet these appropriately to promote children's growth and development.

Points to consider to meet Standard 8

8.1 Drinking water

Fresh drinking water can be made freely available to children in a variety of ways, such as covered jugs, water fountains, cooled water units or bottled water.

Children need regular drinks. You should be alert and responsive to this by:

- making children aware that drinking water is available to them at all times
- assisting children to help themselves where appropriate
- providing suitable bottles, mugs and cups for the ages of the children
- encouraging children to ask for a drink
- offering children drinks regularly
- monitoring individual children's drinking.

Other factors affect how much children need to drink, such as the temperature indoors and outside, energetic play activities, illness and some types of medication.

8.2 Meals

When offering meals, drinks and snacks to children think about your arrangements for:

- providing healthy and nutritious meals and snacks for all children
- accommodating special dietary needs and preferences
- involving children and parents in planning menus
- organising meal times. For example, staff sitting with children, grouping of children (ages, family groups) and encouraging independence such as choices, self-service
- meeting the needs of children who arrive early in the morning or leave late in the afternoon
- providing suitable utensils, plates, cups and bottles.

8.3 Information from parents

When complying with parents' wishes about food and drink consider:

- children's feelings. For example, they may feel uncomfortable about their particular needs.
- obtaining information and advice regarding special diets and food allergies
- ways of ensuring staff are fully informed.

8.4 Food and drink provided by parents

It is helpful to discuss with parents who provide food and drink for their children the importance of:

- providing safe foods, taking into account the storage facilities available
- suitable implements and containers, such as cool boxes.

You also need to consider your arrangements if parents forget to bring lunch, do not provide enough food or children do not eat what is provided.

You may find it helpful to inform parents of procedures and policies regarding food and drink, such as checking lunchboxes for 'unsafe' items, bearing in mind that food swapping may occur among children, some of whom may have allergies.

What the Inspector looks for:

- Children's records indicating their dietary needs
- Your arrangements for providing food and drink
- How you find out about and meet children's dietary needs
- The arrangements you make when parents provide food and drink for their child.

The Inspector bases judgements on the extent to which:

- children have access to fresh drinking water
- drinks are provided regularly, especially where children are unable to ask for one
- children know they can have a drink if they want one
- staff are aware when children need to drink, for example, after physical play
- all relevant staff are aware of children with special dietary needs, and these needs are sensitively cared for
- if snacks and meals are provided, these are healthy and nutritious.

Good sources of vitamins and minerals

This Appendix shows a number of foods and drinks which are important sources of certain vitamins and minerals. These are based on average servings.

	EXCELLENT	GOOD	USEFUL
VITAMIN A	liver* liver sausage/pâté* carrots spinach sweet potatoes red peppers mango canteloupe melon dried apricots	nectarine peach blackcurrants fresh or canned apricots watercress tomatoes cabbage (dark) broccoli Brussels sprouts runner beans broad beans margarine butter cheese kidney	canned salmon herrings egg honeydew melon prunes orange sweetcorn peas whole milk
VITAMIN D	fortified breakfast cereals herrings pilchards sardines tuna canned salmon egg	liver* (other than chicken liver) liver sausage/pâté* margarine	chicken liver* malted-style drinks
THIAMIN	liver and liver pâté* pork, bacon and ham fortified breakfast cereals malted drinks	wholemeal bread yeast extract oatcakes currant buns nuts potatoes	lean meat chicken and other poultry eggs white or brown bread semi-sweet biscuits
RIBOFLAVIN	liver* kidney	milk malted drinks fortified breakfast cereals almonds	lean meat or poultry bacon mackerel, tuna, salmon sardines, pilchards cheese yoghurt eggs
NIACIN	fortified breakfast cereals canned salmon, tuna pilchards chicken	lean meat sausages kidneys herrings sardines	wholemeal bread peanut butter yeast extract bacon liver sausage*

	EXCELLENT	GOOD	USEFUL
VITAMIN B$_6$	whole grain cereals red meat poultry liver* oily fish	potatoes bananas nuts dried fruit white fish	baked beans lentils and other pulses green vegetables tomatoes wholemeal bread cheese
VITAMIN B$_{12}$	liver* kidney oily fish	beef lamb pork turkey white fish eggs	chicken milk cheese yoghurt marmite ribena bran flakes
FOLATE	most fortified breakfast cereals, eg. cornflakes, bran flakes, crisped rice liver* spinach	yeast extract cabbage Brussels sprouts broccoli peas orange melon kidney	wholemeal bread/flour wheat bisks cauliflower beef runner beans tomatoes parsnip potatoes green leafy salads ackee peanuts
VITAMIN C	blackcurrants orange (and orange juice) strawberries canned guava spring greens green and red peppers (raw)	broccoli cabbage cauliflower spinach tomato Brussels sprouts watercress kiwi fruit mango grapefruit	potatoes green beans peas satsumas eating apples nectarines peaches raspberries blackberries
IRON	fortified breakfast cereals liver* kidney liver sausage/pâté*	wholemeal bread/flour wheat bisks beef beefburger corned beef lamb sardines, pilchards soya beans chick peas lentils spinach broccoli spring greens dried apricots raisins	white bread baked beans broad beans black-eyed peas blackcurrants salmon tuna herrings sausage chicken and other poultry egg tofu
CALCIUM	green leafy vegetables sardines cheese tofu	pilchards yoghurt milk (all types) soya drink fortified with calcium cheese spread sesame seeds sesame paste ground almonds	canned salmon muesli white bread/flour peas, beans, lentils dried fruit orange egg yolk

* Liver, including liver pâté, is very rich in vitamin A which can be harmful in large amounts (see page 27.)
It is recommended that these foods are given to children no more than once a week.[1]

	EXCELLENT	GOOD	USEFUL
ZINC	liver* kidney lean meat corned beef	bacon ham poultry canned sardines shrimps and prawns tofu whole grain breakfast cereals, eg. puffed wheat, bran flakes, wheat bisks nuts	sausages cold cooked meats canned tuna or pilchards eggs milk cheese beans and lentils brown or wholemeal bread plain popcorn sesame seeds
FIBRE (non-starch polysaccharides – NSP)	whole grain or wholewheat breakfast cereals such as bran flakes, wheat bisks, shreddies, shredded wheat, sultana bran wholemeal breads baked beans, chick peas, kidney beans (and most beans) lentils dried apricots, figs, prunes	muesli wholemeal pasta brown breads white bread with added fibre baked potato with skin sweet potato broad beans fresh or frozen peas sweetcorn broccoli Brussels sprouts quorn blackberries dried dates almonds hazelnuts	puffed wheat cereal brown rice white pitta bread pizza potatoes yam houmous canned peas cabbage carrots plantain banana mango raisins sunflower seeds potato crisps

* Liver, including liver pâté, is very rich in vitamin A which can be harmful in large amounts (see page 27.)
It is recommended that these foods are given to children no more than once a week.[1]

Reference

1 Scientific Advisory Committee on Nutrition. 2005. *Review of Dietary Advice on Vitamin A*. London: TSO.

Dietary Reference Values for energy and nutrients for under-5s

In 1991 the Department of Health Committee on Medical Aspects of Food and Nutrition Policy (COMA) published Dietary Reference Values which define the amounts of energy and nutrients that would meet the daily needs of most people in the UK.[1] The Dietary Reference Values include 'Estimated Average Requirements', and 'Reference Nutrient Intakes'. These terms are explained below.

Dietary Reference Values (DRVs)

Dietary Reference Values (DRVs) are benchmark intakes of energy and nutrients. They indicate the amount of energy or individual nutrients needed by a group of people of a certain age range (and sometimes gender) for good health. They are not designed for working out a diet for an individual; eating less of a nutrient than is recommended cannot tell us that an individual is deficient. However, if more than quite a few people in a group fall below the recommendations, this suggests that some individuals in that population may be at risk of deficiency.

The DRVs for energy are described as the Estimated Average Requirement (EAR). Most other nutrients have an EAR and also a Reference Nutrient Intake (RNI) and a Lower Reference Nutrient Intake (LRNI). These terms are described below.

Estimated Average Requirement (EAR)

The average amount of energy or nutrients needed by a group of people. Half the population will have needs greater than this, and half will have needs below this amount.

Reference Nutrient Intake (RNI)

This is the amount of a nutrient which is enough to meet the dietary requirements of about 97% of a group of people. If people get more than this amount they will almost certainly be getting enough.

Lower Reference Nutrient Intake (LRNI)

This is the amount which is sufficient for the 3% of a group of people with the smallest needs. Most people will have needs greater than this.

Energy

The Estimated Average Requirements (EAR) for energy for children aged 6 months to 4 years – that is how many calories a day they need – are shown below.

Estimated Average Requirements for energy for children under 5 years

Age of child	Estimated Average Requirement in kcal (kJ) per day*	
	Boys	Girls
6 months	760kcal (3,200kJ)	710kcal (2,980kJ)
9 months	880kcal (3,680kJ)	820kcal (3,420kJ)
1 year	960kcal (4,020kJ)	910kcal (3,800kJ)
1^1/2 years	1,080kcal (4,520kJ)	1,020kcal (4,260kJ)
2 years	1,190kcal (4,960kJ)	1,130kcal (4,720kJ)
2^1/2 years	1,280kcal (5,370kJ)	1,230kcal (5,140kJ)
3 years	1,490kcal (6,230kJ)	1,370kcal (5,730kJ)
4 years	1,600kcal (6,730kJ)	1,460kcal (6,120kJ)

* In practice the intakes of energy and of nutrients needs to be averaged over several days to take account of variations in appetite and in the diverse foods in a diet from day to day.

The energy we need every day is determined both by a basic level of requirement to keep our bodies functioning (called the Basal Metabolic Rate or BMR) and by the amount of physical activity that we do (for example moving around, walking, or exercising). People who are inactive have lower energy needs and will eat less food to maintain their body weight. It becomes much harder to get all the nutrients needed for good health if less food is eaten.

Fat and carbohydrate

There are no recommendations for the under-5s in terms of the proportion of energy in the diet which should come from fat and total carbohydrate. If under-5s have too little fat, this may affect their growth and development and their diet may be too low in other essential nutrients. Between the ages of 2 and 5 years children's diets should move towards the recommendations currently made for the over-5s. However, in this report the Caroline Walker Trust argues that diets which provide about 35% of energy from fat are likely to be suitable for children aged 1-4 years (see page 21).

The recommendation currently made to restrict the amount of NME sugars in the diet to no more than 11% of energy intake is, however, appropriate for the under-5s.

Derived nutrient values used for calculating the nutrient-based standards in this report

The energy and nutrient values that have been used to create the nutrient-based standards in this report are based on the current Dietary Reference Values for the UK[1] and additional recommendations on salt intakes.[2]

Energy values are based on the following Dietary Reference Values:

- 1-2 year olds: average for boys and girls at 12 months, 18 months, 24 months and 30 months

- 3-4 year olds: average for boys and girls aged 3 years and 4 years.

Values for other nutrients are based on the following dietary reference values:

- 1-2 year olds: as for 1-3 year olds

- 3-4 year olds: 50% as for 1-3 year olds and 50% as for 4-6 year olds.

The values for children aged 1-4 years are the average of those aged 1-2 and 3-4 years.

Nutrient		1-2 year olds	3-4 year olds	1-4 year olds
Energy	kcals	1,100	1,480	1,290
	MJ	4.6	6.2	5.4
Total fat	g	42.8	57.6	50.2
Carbohydrate	g	146.7	197.3	172.0
Non-milk extrinsic sugars (NME sugars)	g	32.3	43.4	37.8
Protein	g	14.5	17.1	15.8
Iron	mg	6.9	6.5	6.7
Zinc	mg	5.0	5.8	5.4
Calcium	mg	350	400	375
Vitamin A	µg	400	450	425
Vitamin C	mg	30	30	30
Sodium	mg	800	1,000	900
Salt	g	2	2.5	2.3

References

1 Department of Health. 1991. *Dietary Reference Values for Food Energy and Nutrients for the United Kingdom. Report on Health and Social Subjects No. 41*. London: HMSO.

2 Scientific Advisory Committee on Nutrition. 2003. *Salt and Health*. London: TSO.

Food-related customs

This is a guide to some of the differences in food choice commonly observed by those from different religious and cultural groups. It is important to emphasise that there may be individual differences in food choices between families, and those providing child care should not make assumptions about anyone's food preferences. It is important to find out about each child from his or her parent or guardian.

	Jewish	Hindu[1]	Sikh[1]	Muslim	Buddhist	Rastafarian[2]
Eggs	No blood spots	It varies	Yes	Yes	It varies	It varies
Milk/yoghurt	Not with meat	Yes	Yes	Yes	Yes	It varies
Cheese	Not with meat	Yes	Yes	It varies	Yes	It varies
Chicken	Kosher	It varies	It varies	Halal	No	It varies
Mutton/lamb	Kosher	It varies	It varies	Halal	No	It varies
Beef and beef products	Kosher	No	No	Halal	No	It varies
Pork and pork products	No	Rarely	Rarely	No	No	No
Fish	With fins and scales	With fins and scales	It varies	It varies	It varies	Yes
Shellfish	No	It varies	It varies	It varies	No	No
Butter/ghee	Kosher	Yes	Yes	Yes	No	It varies
Lard	No	No	No	No	No	No
Cereal foods	Yes	Yes	Yes	Yes	Yes	Yes
Nuts/pulses	Yes	Yes	Yes	Yes	Yes	Yes
Fruits/vegetables	Yes	Yes[3]	Yes	Yes	Yes	Yes
Fasting[4]	Yes	Yes	Yes	Yes	Yes	Yes

1 Strict Hindus and Sikhs will not eat eggs, meat, fish, and some fats.

2 Some Rastafarians are vegan.

3 Jains have restrictions on some vegetable foods. Check with the individuals.

4 Fasting is unlikely to apply to young children.

Useful addresses and further information

Useful addresses

4Children (formerly Kids' Club Network)
City Reach
5 Greenwich View Place
London E14 9NN
T: 020 7512 2112
E: info@4Children.org.uk
www.4children.org.uk

Anaphylaxis Campaign
PO Box 275
Farnborough
Hampshire GU14 4SX
T: 01252 377140
www.anaphylaxis.org.uk

Association of Breastfeeding Mothers
PO Box 207
Bridgwater
Somerset TA6 7YT
T: 0870 401 7711
E: info@abm.me.uk
www.abm.me.uk

BLISS (The Premature Baby Charity)
68 South Lambeth Road
London SW8 1RL
T: 020 7820 9471
E: information@bliss.org.uk
www.bliss.org.uk

Breastfeeding Network
PO Box 11126
Paisley PA2 8YB
Scotland
T: 0870 900 8787
www.breastfeedingnetwork.org.uk

British Allergy Foundation
Deepdene House
30 Bellegrove Road
Welling
Kent DA16 3BY
T: 020 8303 8525
E: allergybaf@compuserve.com
www.allergyfoundation.com

British Dental Association
64 Wimpole Street
London W1N 8AL
T: 020 7935 0875
www.bda.org

British Dietetic Association (Paediatric Group)
5th Floor, Charles House
148-9 Great Charles Street
Queensway
Birmingham B3 3HT
T: 0121 200 8080
E: info@bda.uk.com
www.bda.uk.com

British Heart Foundation
14 Fitzhardinge Street
London W1H 6DH
T: 020 7935 0185
Heart Information Line: 08450 70 80 70
www.bhf.org.uk

British Nutrition Foundation
High Holborn House
52-54 High Holborn
London WC1V 6RQ
T: 020 7404 6504
E: postbox@nutrition.org.uk
www.nutrition.org.uk

Chartered Institute of Environmental Health
Chadwick Court
15 Hatfields
London SE1 8DJ
T: 020 7928 6006
E: centresupport@chgl.com
www.cieh.org.uk

Coeliac UK
Suites A-D Octagon Court
High Wycombe
Buckinghamshire HP11 2HS
T: 01494 437278
www.coeliac.org.uk

Community Practitioners' and Health Visitors' Association (CPHVA)
33-37 Moreland Street
London EC1V 8HA
T: 020 7780 4000
E: infocphva@amicustheunion.org
www.msfcphva.org

Daycare Trust
21 St George's Road
London SE1 6ES
T: 020 7840 3350
E: info@daycaretrust.org.uk
www.daycaretrust.org.uk

Diabetes UK
Macleod House
10 Parkway
London NW1 7AA
T: 020 7424 1000
E: info@diabetes.org.uk
www.diabetes.org.uk

The Food Commission
94 White Lion Street
London N1 9PF
T: 020 7837 2250
E: enquiries@foodcomm.org.uk
www.foodcomm.org.uk

Food Standards Agency
www.food.gov.uk
See also page 85 for details of resources available from the Food Standards Agency.

Health Promotion Agency for Northern Ireland
18 Ormeau Avenue
Belfast BT2 8HS
T: 028 9031 1611
E: info@hpani.org.uk
www.healthpromotionagency.org.uk

La Leche League
BM 3424
London WC1N 3XX
T: 020 7242 1278
www.lalecheleague.org

Learning Through Landscapes
3rd floor
Southside Offices
The Law Courts
Winchester SO23 9DL

The Maternity Alliance (Closed December 2005)
Maternity Alliance publications can be bought from:
National Childbirth Trust
T: 0870 112 1120
E: shop@nctsales.co.uk
www.nctresources.co.uk

Mudiad Ysgolion Meithrin
(Welsh early years specialists)
Boulevard St Brieuc
Aberystwyth
Ceredigion SY23 1PD
T: 01970 639639
www.mym.co.uk

National Asthma Campaign
Providence House
Providence Place
London N1 0NT
T: 020 7226 2260
Helpline: 0845 701 0203
www.asthma.org.uk

National Childbirth Trust
Alexandra House
Oldham Terrace
London W3 6NH
T: 0870 770 3236
E: enquiries@national-childbirth-trust.co.uk
www.nctpregnancyandbabycare.com

National Childminding Association
Royal Court
81 Tweedy Road
Bromley
Kent BR1 1TG
T: 0845 880 0044
www.ncma.org.uk

National Children's Bureau
8 Wakley Street
London EC1V 7QE
T: 020 7843 6000
www.ncb.org.uk

Early Childhood Unit
T: 020 7843 6080
www.earlychildhood.org.uk

National Council of Voluntary Child Care Organisations
Unit 4
Pride Court
80-82 White Lion Street
London N1 9PF
T: 020 7833 3319
E: office@ncvcco.org
www.ncvcco.org

National Day Nurseries Association
Oak House
Woodvale Road
Brighouse
West Yorkshire HD6 4AB
T: 0870 774 4244
E: info@ndna.org.uk
www.ndna.org.uk

National Heart Forum
Tavistock House South
Tavistock Square
London WC1H 9LG
T: 020 7383 7638
www.heartforum.org.uk

National Institute for Health and Clinical
Excellence (NICE)
MidCity Place
71 High Holborn
London WC1V 6NA
T: 020 7067 5800
www.publichealth.nice.org.uk

NHS Direct
T: 0845 4647
www.nhsdirect.nhs.uk

NHS Health Scotland
Woodburn House
Canaan Lane
Edinburgh EH10 4SG
T: 0131 536 5500
www.healthscotland.com

Northern Ireland Pre-school Playgroup
Association (NIPPA)
6c Wildflower Way
Belfast BT12 6TA
T: 028 9066 2825
E: info@nippa.org.uk
www.nippa.org

Play Wales/Chwarae Cymru
Baltic House
Mount Stuart Square
Cardiff CF10 5FH
T: 029 2048 6050
E: mail@playwales.org.uk
www.playwales.org.uk

Pre-school Learning Alliance
The Fitzpatrick Building
188 York Way
London N7 9AD
T: 020 7697 2500
www.pre-school.org.uk

Royal College of Paediatrics and Child
Health
50 Hallam Street
London W1W 6DE
T: 020 7307 5600
www.rcpch.ac.uk

The Royal Institute of Public Health and
Hygiene
28 Portland Place
London W1B 1DE
T: 020 7580 2731
www.riph.org.uk

Scottish Pre-school Play Association
45 Finnieston Street
Glasgow G3 8JU
T: 0141 221 4148
www.sppa.org.uk

Vegan Society
Donald Watson House
7 Battle Road
St Leonard's on Sea
East Sussex TN37 7AA
T: 01424 427393
www.vegansociety.com

Vegetarian Society
Parkdale
Dunham Road
Altrincham
Cheshire WA14 4QG
T: 0161 928 0793
www.vegsoc.org

Wales Pre-school Playgroups Association
Ladywell House
Newtown
Powys SY16 1JB
T: 01686 624573
www.walesppa.org.

Working Families
1-3 Berry Street
London EC1V 0AA
T: 020 7253 7243
E: office@workingfamilies.org.uk
www.workingfamilies.org.uk

Further information

Caroline Walker Trust publications

For details see www.cwt.org.uk.

Eating Well for Under-5s in Child Care:
Training Materials for People Working
with Under-5s in Child Care
Training materials on eating well and
practical menu planning advice for use by
individual child carers, or by those offering
training to owners, managers, catering
staff, local authority staff, childminders,
teachers and other carers in environments
providing child care for infants and under-
5s. The materials include a CD-ROM with
useful information about foods, recipes and
menu planning.

Eating Well at School
Nutritional and practical guidelines for food
served in schools throughout the day to
children aged 5-18 years.

Eating Well for Looked After Children and
Young People
Nutritional and practical guidelines for food
served to 5-18 year olds who are cared for
in children's homes or by foster carers.

Department of Health publications

Available from:
Department of Health
PO Box 777
London SE1 6XH
T: 0800 555777

Breast Feeding (2004) Leaflet

Bottle Feeding (2005) Leaflet

Weaning (2005) Leaflet

Practical Food Hygiene. Poster in A3 or A2
Sizes

Birth to Five: Your Complete Guide to
Parenthood and the First Five Years of
Your Child's Life (2005 edition)

Welfare Food Scheme: Nursery Milk Guide
for Providers of Day Care for Children
Under Five (2003) Leaflet

For information on the new Healthy Start
scheme see www.healthystart.nhs.uk

Food Standards Agency publications

Available from:
PO Box 369
Hayes
Middlesex UB3 1UT
T: 0845 606 0667
F: 020 8867 3225
Minicom (for people with hearing
disabilities): 0845 606 0678
E: foodstandards@eclogistics.co.uk

Be Allergy Aware FSA0002

Ten Tips for Food Safety FSA0006

The Food Safety Act 1990 and You
FSA0238. Booklet summarising the Food
Safety Act.

The Balance of Good Health
FSA/0008/0604

Healthy Diets for Infants and Young
Children FSA0249

Feeding Your Baby FSA/0454/0602

Feeding Your Toddler FSA/0455/0105

Feeding Your Growing Child
FSA/0456/0602

Further information on healthy eating can
be obtained from:
www.eatwell.gov.uk
www.salt.gov.uk
www.food.gov.uk

National Children's Bureau publication

www.ncb-books.org.uk

Child Development from Birth to Eight: A
Practical Focus
A book for all who work with children but
need to know more about how children
learn and develop.
ISBN 1 904787 282

NHS Health Scotland/Scottish Executive publications

www.healthscotland.com/publications

Nutritional Guidance for Early Years: Food Choices for Children Aged 1-5 Years in Early Education and Childcare Settings
Scottish Executive, 2006
Orders: 0131 622 8283
E: business.edinburgh@blackwell.co.uk
ISBN 0755947878

Adventures in Foodland 2005
Nutrition resource aimed at carers of pre-school children, especially carers of very young children in the 0-3 age group.
1-84485-113-3

Fun First Foods 2005
Provides tips, advice, recipes and information on the different stages of weaning.
1-84485-274-1

Is your Child a Fussy Eater? Leaflet (2003)

It's Never Too Early to Think about Your Baby's Teeth Flyer (1998)

Mothers Caring for Young Children's Teeth Flyer (1997)

Health Promotion Agency (Northern Ireland) publications

www.healthpromotionagency.org.uk/resources
T: 028 9031 1611
F: 028 9031 1711

Off to a Good Start: All You Need to Know about Breastfeeding Your Baby (2004)
Contains essential facts to help mothers in making informed choices about how to feed their babies.
1-84485-283-0

Weaning Made Easy: Moving from Milk to Family Meals (2005)
For parents of young babies and health professionals working with this group.

Food 4 Play Pack (2005)
Presented in three sections: *Eating for Health, Food Activity Pack,* and *Good Practice.*

Getting a Good Start – Healthy Eating from One to Five (2004)
This booklet outlines advice on many key nutritional issues for children aged 1-5.

Nutrition Matters for the Early Years – Guidance for Feeding Under Fives in the Childcare Setting (2005)

Publications from the Welsh Assembly

Bilingual resources (in English and Welsh) have been produced by the Welsh Assembly Government and can be downloaded as PDF files from:
www.cmo.wales.gov.uk/content/publications/index-e.htm

Weaning booklets:

Help ... My Child is Fussy with Food

Stage 1: Easy to Cook Family Foods for Your Baby

Stage 2: Easy to Cook Family Foods for Your Baby

Stage 3: Easy to Cook Family Foods for Your Baby

Publications from the British Dietetic Association Paediatric Group

www. bda.uk.com

After Milk – What's Next? (2004)

Help – My Child Won't Eat! (2004)

Food for the Growing Years (2004)

Food for the School Years (2004)

National Childbirth Trust publications

Available from: www.nctms.co.uk

NCT Book of Breastfeeding
Mary Smale (1999)
Harper Collins
ISBN 0007136080

Breastfeeding – How to Express and Store Your Milk
Booklet (2000)

Successful Breastfeeding
Royal College of Midwives (2001)
Churchill Livingstone
ISBN 0443059675

Publications from BLISS, the Premature Baby Charity

www.bliss.org.uk
(Address on page 84.)

Breastfeeding Your Premature Baby (2005) Leaflet

Weaning Your Premature Baby (2003) Leaflet

Equipment

Both of the following are available from: www.nctms.co.uk

Doidy cups
Doidy cups are specially designed to help young children drink from a cup.

Weaning cubes
For freezing or storing baby food or breast milk.

Cookery books

365 Recipes for Babies, Toddlers and Children
Bridget Wardley and Judy More
Duncan Baird
ISBN 1 84483 036 5

Baby and Child Vegetarian Recipes
Carol Timperley
Ebury Press, London
ISBN 0091853001

Dump The Junk
Mary Whiting and Ben Nash
Moonscape Ltd
ISBN 0954432401

Finger Food for Babies and Toddlers
Jennie Malzells
Vermillion
ISBN 0091889510

First Foods and Weaning
Ravinder Lilly
Harper Collins
ISBN 0007136072

The Nursery Food Book
Mary Whiting and Tim Lobstein
Arnold (Hodder Headline)
ISBN 0340718943

Food customs

Celebration!
Barnabas and Annabel Kindersley
Dorling Kindersley Ltd, London
ISBN 0 7513 5650 6

Festivals and Celebrations
Jim Fitzsimmons and Rhona Whiteford
Scholastic Educational Books
ISBN 0 590 53083 6

'SHAP' calendar of religious festivals
A calendar of festivals for the current year.
Available from:
SHAP Working Party
c/o National Society Religious Education Centre
36 Causton Street
London SW1P 4AU
T: 020 7932 1194
www.shap.org.uk

Learning through play

Clay and Dough
Lynne Burgess
Scholastic Educational Books
ISBN 0 590 53638 9

Food
Lesley Clark
In the 'Themes for Early Years' series.
Scholastic Educational Books
ISBN 0 590 53719 9

Food and Cooking – Ready, Steady, Play
Sandy Green
David Fulton (2004)
ISBN 184312100X

Fun Outdoors
Fun with Role Play
Fun with Games
Booklets for parents and carers aimed at 3-5 year olds.
The Basic Skills Agency
www.basic-skills.co.uk

The Little Book of Dough
Lynn Garner, Melanie Roan, Marion Taylor and Sally Featherstone
Featherstone Education
ISBN 1905019106

Snack Time
Jenni Clark
Featherstone Education (2005)
ISBN 1 905019 19 X

ORGANISATIONS AND WEBSITES

The Children's Play Council
www.ncb.org.uk/cpc

Early Years Outdoors
www.ltl.org.uk
Dedicated early years service from Learning through Landscapes offers resources to encourage outdoor play.

Sources of resource material for food-related activities

Catalogues are available from the following companies.

ASCO Educational Supplies Ltd
19 Lockwood Way
Parkside Lane
Leeds LS11 5TH
T: 0113 270 7070
E: sales@ascoeducational.co.uk
www.ascoeducational.co.uk

Early Learning Centre
South Marston Park
Swindon SN3 4TJ
T: 0870 535 2352
www.elc.co.uk

The Festival Shop Ltd
56 Poplar Road
Kings Heath
Birmingham B14 7AG
T: 0121 444 0444
E: web@festivalshop.co.uk
www.festivalshop.co.uk

Hope Education
Hyde Building
Ashton Road
Hyde
Cheshire SK14 4SH
T: 0845 120 2224
E: enquiries@hope-education.co.uk
www.hope-education.co.uk

Pictorial Charts Educational Trust
27 Kirchen Road
London W13 OUD
T: 020 8567 9206
E: info@pcet.co.uk
www.pcet.co.uk

Schofield and Sims Ltd
Dogley Mill
Fenay Bridge
Huddersfield
West Yorkshire HD8 0NQ
T: 01484 607080
E: post@schofieldandsims.co.uk
www.schofieldandsims.co.uk

Scholastic UK
Westfield Road
Southam CV33 0JH
T: 01926 813910
E: enquiries@scholastic.co.uk
www.scholastic.co.uk

Training in 'Eating Well' for early years care providers

In the UK, registered dietitians (RD) and registered public health nutritionists (RPHNutr) are the professionals qualified to provide advice and training on good nutrition in public settings.

Registered dietitians can be found via the British Dietetic Association:
www.bda.uk.com

Registered public health nutritionists can be found via the Nutrition Society:
www.nutritionsociety.org

The *Eating Well for Under 5s: Training Materials* which accompany this report (see page 85) provide the contact details of individuals around the UK who are suitably qualified and who are willing to offer training to early years settings. For an up-to-date list of trainers, see www.cwt.org.uk

Index

A
activities: food-related 57
activity 9, 20, 46
allergies 38, 52
atmosphere at eating times 11, 55
awards: healthy eating awards 60

B
B vitamins 29, 78
behaviour and diet 53
bottle feeds 39, 43
breakfast 11, 54
breastfeeding 12, 38

C
calcium 34, 52, 79
calories 20, 81
carbohydrates 22, 69, 81
carer involvement in meals 55
carotene 27
celebrations 58
childcare places 15
constipation 25
copper 35
cups for infants 42, 50
customs related to food 83

D
dairy-free diets 52
dental health 10, 23, 49, 50
diarrhoea 25
Dietary Reference Values 81
disabilities: children with 53
drinks: for infants 12, 42
   for under-5s 9, 46, 49
DRVs 81

E
EAR 81
energy (calories) 20, 81
equal opportunities 12, 46
erosion of teeth 50
Estimated Average Requirement 81
exercise 9, 20, 46

F
fat in the diet 21, 62, 81
fatness in children 20, 47
festivals 58
fibre 25, 80
fish 45, 70, 71
five a day 31
folate 29, 79
food groups 45, 69
food policy 59
food safety: infants 13, 43
   under-5s 10, 53
fruit 30, 31, 45, 69
fruit drinks 42, 49
full-day care 64

G
groups: food groups 45, 69

H
half-day care 64

I
infant formula 39
infant nutrition 38
intrinsic sugars 22
iodine 35
iron 32, 41, 63, 79

J
juice 42, 49

L
learning through food 11, 56
listening: to children 57
   to parents 11, 57
liver 27

M
magnesium 35
mealtimes 54, 55, 56
meat 32, 70
menus 57, 71, 72
milk products 45, 70
milk: for babies 12, 38
   for under-5s 47, 70
minerals 32, 78

N
n-3 polyunsaturated fats 21
niacin 29, 78
NMES 23
non-milk extrinsic sugars 23
non-starch polysaccharides 25, 80
NSP 25, 80
nutrient-based standards 8, 61, 65
nutrition policy 59
nuts 53

O
obesity 20, 47
omega-3 fats 21

P
parents: involving parents 11, 57
phosphorus 36
physical activity 9, 20, 46
policy: nutrition policy 59
polyunsaturated fats 21
potassium 36
prebiotics/probiotics 25
protein 24

R
recommendations 8
   for menu planners 69
Reference Nutrient Intakes 24, 81
refusal of food 56
retinol 27
rewards 55

S
safety of foods: see 'food safety'
salt 34, 63
sample menus 72
saturated fat 21
selenium 36
snacks 11, 45, 54, 55, 64
social skills 11
sodium 34, 63
soft drinks 49
special diets 52
special needs 53
standards: nutrient-based 8, 61, 65
starchy foods 22, 69
sugars 22, 49, 50
supplements 21, 53
sustainability 11, 71

T
tea (beverage) 32, 49
teeth: see dental health
thiamin 29, 78
timing: of feeds for infants 40
   of meals and snacks 11, 54
tooth erosion 50
toothbrushing 51
training 8, 87

V
variety of foods 44
vegan diets 52
vegetables 31, 45, 69
vegetarian diets 33, 51, 73
vitamin A 26, 27, 78
vitamin B6 26, 30, 79
vitamin B12 26, 30, 79
vitamin C 26, 30, 32, 79
vitamin D 26, 28, 42, 63, 71, 78
vitamin drops 28, 41, 52
vitamin E 26
vitamin K 26
vitamins 26, 78

W
water 49
   for babies 40, 42
weaning 13, 40, 42

Z
zinc 34, 63, 80

riboflavin 29, 78
RNI 24, 81